W9-ASH-428

The Cold War in Transition

The Cold War in Transition

David S. McLellan
UNIVERSITY OF CALIFORNIA, RIVERSIDE

The Macmillan Company, New York
Collier–Macmillan Limited, London

Third Printing, 1967

Library of Congress catalog card number: 66–15371

THE MACMILLAN COMPANY, NEW YORK
COLLIER–MACMILLAN CANADA, LTD., TORONTO, ONTARIO

PRINTED IN THE UNITED STATES OF AMERICA

To My Mother and Father

I wish to thank my colleagues, Dr. Morton Schwartz, Dr. Fred Sondermann, Norman Cherniss, and Robert McLellan, for their criticism and suggestions for improving the manuscript. It would doubtless have been a better manuscript had I been able to incorporate all of their recommendations. I would also like to thank my students, John Reuss and Joel Blain for research assistance and Joyce Edwards and Florence Foulke for typing the manuscript and relieving me of other chores.

Contents

CHAPTER 1

From Alliance to Cold War

EVEN BEFORE WORLD WAR II had ended, the victors were competing to achieve the best possible postwar position. As long as a powerful common enemy remained in the field, the great coalition held together. The common interest in defeating the Axis states transcended and muted the latent rivalry and conflict between the Soviet Union and the two leading Western powers, Great Britain and the United States. Whatever the wartime cooperation had done to reduce the basic hostility that had previously marked Soviet relations with the leading democratic and capitalist states, the common heroism and sacrifices could not submerge the basic relationship that East and West were destined to assume toward one another.

Rivalry is endemic to the nation-state system. The nature of the system compels every participant to provide its own security; and one nation's security is another nation's insecurity. The logic of the nation-state system breeds insecurity, distrust, rivalry, and hostility. In theory all members are enemy to the others, but in practice the international system at any given time does not generally comprise all nations attracting and repelling each other at random.

Because all nations are not of equal strength or in exactly similar geographic relationships to each other, or uniformly willing to accept the status quo, individual nation-states sometimes modify the degree of hostility toward certain other nation-states in order to band together to enhance their security against another seemingly threatening single state or cluster of states. This pattern sometimes illustrates the statement, "The enemy of my enemy is my friend." Or two rivals may seek to make an alliance with the state on the opponent's other border. Thus France, fearful of Germany, sought to ally itself before World War I with Tsarist Russia and following World War I with the newly independent states on Germany's eastern borderland: Poland, Czechoslovakia, Yugoslavia, and Rumania. Another pattern was illustrated when Great Britain, confronted by the emergence of Wilhelmian Germany as both a naval rival and as a threat to European balance of power after 1890, relinquished its ambitions in the Caribbean in favor of the United States and in the area of Manchuria in favor of Japan.

Rivalry is also endemic to the nation-state system for psychological reasons. Citizens and nations seek to establish their identity, a process that often manifests itself in hostility toward others. This anxiety and hostility is always seeking an object. The nature of the nation-state system and the mechanisms of ethnocentrism directly interact to reinforce each other. This reaction invariably reinforces the relationship of hostility and rivalry born of the security dilemma. This process may build up to a military eruption or it may subside, but patterns of conflict and hostility are an enduring aspect of relations between nation-states.

The postwar relationship of the United States and the Soviet Union was conducive to just such an outcome. The principal consequence of Hitler's attack upon Russia had been to destroy the balance set up in 1919 between Central Europe and Bolshevist Russia and to open the way for Soviet power to flood over Eastern and Central Europe. Similarly, the Japanese conquest of China and Southeast Asia sped the erosion of the status quo in those regions by undermining Europe hegemony and igniting revolutionary nationalism.

As the war ended, Soviet and American power confronted each other over congeries of prostrate, exhausted, and chaotic societies that provided an invitation to rivalry. Had Germany and Japan not been reduced to impotence by unconditional surrender or had France, Britain, and China been able to maintain control of their traditional spheres of influence, the Soviet-American confrontation might have been somewhat less stark and threatening. For a time the United States believed that the British Empire would continue to play its traditional role in the vast belt of land and sea stretching from Gibraltar to Singapore, an illusion that was soon shattered. Unfortunately, the historical magnitude and consequences of the war were destined to cast Russia and America in the fatal role of antagonists with no third state powerful enough to balance and relieve the acute security dilemma.

The enormous destruction wrought upon the Soviet Union by the German juggernaut was bound to produce a quest for maximum security guarantees. Russia lost 13.6 million soldiers and "the military campaigns in the Soviet Union devastated 1,710 cities and settlements, 70,000 towns and villages, and over 6 million buildings of all kinds."[1]

The government of any nation suffering such staggering losses would be bound to seek to take measures against any such catastrophe

[1] Jacobsen, Hans-Adolf, "The Second World War as a Problem in Historical Research," *World Politics,* July 1964, p. 640.

ever again occurring.[2] The Soviet Union engaged in a supreme wartime effort to conquer as much of the vital borderlands as possible. As long as this effort also served the common purpose of defeating the Axis, its implications for the future were passed over in silence or veiled with some ambiguous and face-saving formula by Roosevelt and Churchill. But as victory drew near, the necessity for suppressing the security dilemma implicit in Soviet expansion lessened.

At first subtly and then more and more openly the British and American leaders began to challenge the legitimacy of Soviet activities in Eastern Europe. Between the Yalta and Potsdam Conferences (February and June 1945) a critical transformation occurred in the expectations between Russia and the West.[3] "For during the discussion of ways and means of remolding Europe politically in order to ensure peace in the world and in the wake of unilateral measures in Eastern Europe, the alliance fell apart. The ideological chasm which until then had been concealed by the Soviet Union and disregarded or minimized by the Western nations was too deep."[4]

The United States was content during the closing months of the war and the first months of the postwar period to preserve those advantages with which it was emerging from the war. Even before his death, Roosevelt had reversed himself on Germany. Instead of going forward with either the "Morgenthau Plan" or other plans for the dismemberment of Germany, he and Churchill refused to commit themselves "to Russian proposals for Germany that would unavoidably magnify Soviet power in Europe."[5] On the last day of the Yalta conference, Secretary of State Edward Stettinius, Foreign Minister V. M. Molotov, and Foreign Secretary Anthony Eden signed a revised clause on Germany that read as follows:

> The United Kingdom, the United States of America and the Union of Soviet Socialist Republics shall possess supreme authority with respect to Germany. In the exercise of such authority they will take such steps, including the complete disarmament, demilitarisation and the dismemberment of Germany *as they deem requisite* for future peace and security.[6]

[2] Djilas reports a conversation with Stalin while the war was still on: "That Germany is a highly developed industrial country with an extremely qualified and numerous working class and technical intelligentsia. Give them twelve to fifteen years and they'll be on their feet again. . . . We shall recover in fifteen or twenty years, and then we'll have another go at it." Djilas, Milovan, *Conversations with Stalin* (New York: Harcourt, Brace & World, 1962), pp. 114–115.

[3] Snell, John, *Illusion and Necessity* (Boston: Houghton Mifflin, 1963), pp. 172–191.

[4] Jacobsen, *op. cit.*, p. 635.

[5] Snell, *op. cit.*, p. 187.

[6] *Ibid.*, p. 190.

Stalin and Molotov left Yalta fully conscious that a turning point had been reached in Soviet-Western relations.

On May 9, acknowledging Germany's surrender to the U.S.S.R., Stalin himself proclaimed that the Soviet Union did not intend "either to dismember or to destroy Germany." Asked later that month why he had changed his mind, Stalin told Hopkins that "subsequent events had shown that the proposal in regard to dismembering had really been rejected at the Crimea Yalta Conference"; that in the special committee studying the question the British representative, "without objection" by the American member, "had interpreted the Crimea Decision not as a positive plan for the dismembering of Germany but as a threat to hold over the Germans' head in the event of bad behavior." Stalin ruefully added that "after Yalta the British press had consistently said that only Russia was for the dismemberment of Germany."[7]

Between the Yalta Conference and the Potsdam Conference, diplomatic sparring between East and West intensified as each side openly maneuvered to be in a position of maximum advantage at the war's end. Both sides were content to preserve the fiction of cooperation but neither really believed that it could afford to trust the other. However, the United States still did not have the inclination or the incentive to challenge Soviet activities in Eastern Europe because it was obviously dependent on Soviet assistance in the Far East and was still hoping that nothing would interfere with a return to normalcy.

Truman lacked Roosevelt's incentive to avoid a rupture with the master of the Kremlin. Almost from the beginning he regarded Soviet breaches of agreement as just that—breaches of agreement. He did not need to ask whether the ideological terms and the political aims they proclaimed, such as "peace," "freedom," and "democracy," meant the same in the East as in the West.

Truman could see that the consequences of Soviet actions posed difficult problems for the United States, and he was personally convinced that further concessions would only worsen rather than improve the Western position. Consequently, without adopting any consistent or purposeful course of action, Truman nevertheless refused to make any more concessions for the sake of preserving amicable relations or to concede anything that was not already within the Soviet orbit of power. As cooperation between Soviet and Western powers weakened, the relationship inevitably turned into competition and rivalry. The Soviet Union was guided by a view of

[7] *Ibid.*

history that postulated the inevitability of a hostile international environment as long as capitalist states existed.

In the first months of the postwar period each of the great victors acted consistently with their wartime behavior. The Soviet Union sought to consolidate its control over those societies that had come within its military grip; the British and French endeavored to regain control over lost parts of their empires and to recover economically; and the United States began to retreat into its traditional political and military noninvolvement.

This uneasy state of affairs did not last long. No one of the principal victors could act within its own sphere without its actions appearing hostile to the other two. By its very nature, state action usually seeks to enhance the stability and security and therefore the power of the state. The accretion of power by one member can only appear threatening and therefore hostile to the other states in the system. Thus Soviet efforts to consolidate its power in Eastern Europe appeared threatening to Western Europe. Secretary of State James Byrnes' "get tough" line and the hard bargaining with which he opposed Soviet designs in Eastern Europe seemed to strike at Russia's hard-won security interests. Because of their Marxist-Leninist view of the world, the Soviet leaders were especially prone to view Anglo-American strictures as fundamentally hostile toward Russia. Their conception of security required Communist governments in Eastern Europe. For the United States to challenge the legitimacy of those governments was tantamount to challenging Russia's security.

As early as August 1945, President Mikhail Kalinin warned a meeting of the Moscow Communist Party that the Soviet Union was the "one socialist state in the world" and that "the perils of capitalist encirclement had not disappeared with Hitlerite Germany." Molotov amplified this in a speech on November 6, 1945, when he told a meeting of the Moscow Soviet that the "roots of fascism and imperialist aggression" had not been "finally extirpated."[8]

Finally on February 9, 1946, Stalin reaffirmed the thesis of basic capitalist ill-will and hostility, by declaring that the "capitalist system of world economy" conceals within itself "the elements of general crisis and military clashes."

> "It would be wrong," Stalin declared, "to think that the Second World War was a casual occurrence or the result of mistakes . . . actually the war was the inevitable result of the development of world economic and

[8] Warth, Robert D., *Soviet Russia in World Politics* (New York: Twayne, 1963), p. 320.

political forces on the basis of modern monopoly capitalism. Marxists have declared more than once that the capitalist system harbors elements of general crises and armed conflicts and that, hence the development of world capitalism proceeds . . . through crises and military conflicts."[9]

These words were received with foreboding by Western leaders. But certainly Anglo-American leaders at the same time viewed Soviet actions as fundamentally hostile to Western interests. Soviet obstructionism and resistance to American demands concerning Eastern Europe prompted an unabashedly hostile response from President Truman that reflected the mood of a growing number of Americans. Incensed by Secretary Byrnes' failure to consult with him adequately and with his apparently conciliatory attitude toward Russia in the course of the December Foreign Ministers Meeting in Moscow, Truman bluntly ordered Byrnes to adopt a "tough line."

There isn't a doubt in my mind that Russia intends an invasion of Turkey and the seizure of the Black Sea Straits to the Mediterranean. Unless Russia is faced with an iron fist and strong language another war is in the making. Only one language do they understand—"how many divisions have you?"

I do not think we should play compromise any longer. We should refuse to recognize Rumania and Bulgaria until they comply with our requirements; we should let our position on Iran be known in no uncertain terms and we should continue to insist on the internationalization of the Kiel Canal, the Rhine-Danube waterway and the Black Sea Straits and we should maintain complete control of Japan and the Pacific. We should rehabilitate China and create a strong central government there. We should do the same for Korea.

Then we should insist on the return of our ships from Russia and force a settlement of the Lend-Lease debt of Russia.

I'm tired of babying the Soviets.[10]

Within six months after the war's end all pretense at friendship was being dropped. Henceforth each side would interpret all moves as basically hostile and therefore would act accordingly. The Cold War had begun.

This unexpected development conflicted with the American people's desire to return to the pursuit of their private interests; to retreat into a haven where there were no moral uncertainties of international involvement. Their government might be aware of the menacing

[9] *Ibid.*

[10] Truman, Harry S., *Memoirs* (New York: Doubleday, 1955), Vol. I, pp. 551–552.

ambiguities of the situation, but Americans were determined not to let their growing disenchantment with the Soviet Union impede their return to their private concerns. Unfortunately the American government could not for long indulge itself in that pleasant flight from reality.

For a brief period American officials wistfully hoped that Britain would have the strength to play its traditional role as the guardian of its empire running roughly from Gibraltar to Singapore. But the sudden cessation of Lend-Lease on V-J Day disclosed a totally unexpected crisis in Britain's financial ability to carry on its empire. Conditions in France, Italy, and occupied Germany also were far more desperate and chaotic than had been anticipated. Under the circumstances the Administration felt compelled to renew and increase economic and financial assistance to the Europeans and to protect the German situation from needless deterioration. Billion-dollar loans were approved for Britain and France; the Soviet Union's request for a $5 billion loan was pigeonholed in the State Department and no one seriously considered asking the Congress for such a loan. Rightly or wrongly the Soviet Union viewed these and other American policies in support of stability in Europe as part of a conscious effort to reconstitute an anti-Soviet bloc.

Americans were beginning to claim that Soviet machinations were at the root of their wholly unanticipated and exceedingly painful obligation to turn their attention once again to world problems. Instead of merely expressing disagreement, both sides began to challenge the legitimacy of the other's actions. On January 19, 1946, the Iranian delegate lodged a protest with the newly organized United Nations Security Council against the continued occupation of Northern Iran by Russian troops. When the March 2 deadline for the withdrawal of foreign troops found the Red Army still strongly ensconced in Iran, the American as well as British governments registered a protest with Moscow. The Iranian crisis was given added emphasis on March 5, 1946, when former Prime Minister Churchill, speaking at Fulton, Missouri, in the presence of President Truman and other important Americans, denounced the existence of an "Iron Curtain" and invited America to take up the challenge posed by the Russian occupation of Eastern Europe:

> . . . there is nothing they [the Russians] admire so much as strength, and there is nothing for which they have less respect than for weakness.[11]

[11] Trefousse, H. L., editor *The Cold War: A Book of Documents* (New York: Putnams, 1965), p. 81.

Churchill's outspoken frankness was greeted with expressions of general shock and alarm by the presses in the United States and Great Britain. No American official endorsed Churchill's grim assessment of the situation. But in truth Churchill had only publicly proclaimed what high diplomatic officials here and abroad held privately. What they objected to was not the content of Churchill's remarks but his timing. Only the previous month a long cable had been received from a little known American diplomat in Moscow, George F. Kennan. The cable contained a long and thoughtful analysis of the sources of Soviet motivation and conduct in foreign affairs. Kennan attributed Soviet aggressiveness to internal tensions: "At the bottom of the Kremlin's neurotic view of world affairs is the traditional and instinctive Russian sense of insecurity," overlaid with Lenin's sanguinary view of history and reinforced by the nature of Stalin's dictatorship. "These characteristics of Soviet policy are basic to the internal nature of Soviet power, and will be with us, whether in the foreground or the background, until the internal nature of Soviet power is changed." Meanwhile, Kennan warned, Soviet political action "is a fluid stream which moves constantly, wherever it is permitted to move, toward a given goal. Its main concern is to make sure that it has filled every nook and cranny available to it in the basin of world power." American policy in the face of Soviet expansionism must be that "of a long-term, patient but firm and vigilant containment of Russian expansive tendencies." Kennan urged a campaign to educate the American people to the "utter ruthlessness and complete unscrupulousness of [the] Soviet ruling clique."[12]

Events in 1946 emphasized more clearly the contradiction between the diagnosis so ably advanced by Kennan and Churchill and the American desire to return to freedom from international responsibility. Soon the untenability of America's posture began to have repercussions on the domestic scene.

The nature of the demands being placed upon American foreign policy by the rapid intensification of the Cold War was viewed with alarm by two major segments within American society. Within the Cabinet itself, Henry Wallace, former Vice President and now Truman's Secretary of Commerce, viewed the deterioration in Soviet-American relations with horror. Soviet-American collaboration had taken on a mystical quality somewhat akin to world redemption for Wallace and his followers; they felt that anything that interfered with

[12] Kennan, George F., "The Sources of Soviet Conduct," in *American Diplomacy: 1900–1950* (New York: Mentor, 1960), pp. 89–106.

its perpetuation was due not to the impersonal workings of international politics but to personal machinations of British imperialists and Wall Street reactionaries. Wallace was the last spokesman of fervent idealism that flowered under Roosevelt and the New Deal. The war's demand for managerial talent and its general callousing effect had stifled support for the kind of idealism that Wallace espoused. Or perhaps the war and the Cold War left little room for an idealism based on an optimism and humanity that were themselves the product of America's century-long freedom from external threat. Now that the United States confronted the security dilemma in all its diabolic force, naive idealism was bound to wither.

Whatever the cause, Wallace and his followers within the Democratic Party viewed with dismay the shattering consequences of the Cold War upon their dream of one world. Truman could not bring himself to break openly with Wallace; the Cold War did that for him. The crises of the year 1946 caused a steady worsening of Soviet-American relations. Unable to reconcile himself to the failure of his ideals, Wallace finally placed the President in such a position with his Secretary of State that Truman had to ask for Wallace's resignation. Wallace's subsequent criticisms of United States foreign policy and his 1948 campaign for President on the Progressive ticket with Communist backing fed the hysterical anti-Communism of a later phase of the Cold War.

Another influential segment of American society that rejected the implications of the Cold War were the isolationists. During the war isolationists, led by Senator Robert A. Taft, had been forced into the background. With war's end they had hoped to make a comeback, but they realized that if the Cold War were to become a permanent feature of the political landscape, America would never regain its pristine freedom from statism, militarism, and the evils of the world beyond its shores. Isolationists like Taft were just as dismayed by the Cold War as were "one worlders" like Wallace. True, Wallace favored one world and Taft favored America without the rest of the world, but both were opposed to America's pursuing the Cold War and both reacted to each episode with strikingly similar words. Both accused Truman of "pulling British chestnuts out of the fire" in the Middle East and Iran and of provoking the Soviet Union with his statement of the Truman Doctrine in March, 1947.

Although in some way most Americans shared the chagrin of Taft and Wallace, it was easier to blame the Communists for the disturbing situation confronting the nation. The mechanism of ethnocentrism was beginning to work in its peculiarly American way; subtle suggestion was being implanted in American minds that salvation lay in purging American government and society generally of Communists and their dupes.[13]

The Cold War was manifesting itself in a similar fashion in the Soviet Union, where Stalin and Andrei Zhdanov were purging Soviet society and culture of all Western influences that had crept in during an occasional unguarded wartime moment. The necessity to steel the Soviet people for additional sacrifices if Russia was to recover prompted the Kremlin to reinstitute terror and tension as the principal means of eliciting a maximum human effort.

As the Cold War intensified and the full extent of wartime damage to the European and Asian economies became known, it became more and more obvious that only American power could preserve the postwar structure of the international system.

During 1946 the nature of the Cold War shifted from a more or less passive condition to an active one. The Iranian crisis in the spring of 1946 was followed by a crisis over the Dardanelles, the shooting down of United States transports over Yugoslavia, and tense episodes in Trieste and Manchuria. In September, following an unsuccessful Foreign Ministers' conference about a peace treaty for Germany, Secretary Byrnes journeyed to Stuttgart, Germany. There he told assembled representatives of the German people in the American zone of occupation that the United States had no intention of seeing Germany decline into impotence and despair. Byrnes told them that the Army of the United States would be part of the occupation forces, "as long as an occupation force is required in Germany;" that the Oder-Neisse line between Germany and Poland was provisional; that the United States favored German retention of the Rhineland and the Ruhr; and that "the American people want to help the German people to win their way back to an honorable place among the free and peace-loving nations of the world."[14]

The Cold War also spurred the United States to make a vast loan to overcome the economic debilitation of Britain and France. The

[13] On April 1, 1946, a special committee of the Republican National Committee demanded "That the State Department be so reorganized that it may possess cohesion and unity of purpose; that only those persons who believe in the American way of life and are loyal to the American government shall be employed. . . ."

[14] "Stuttgart Speech by J. F. Byrnes, United States Secretary of State Restatement of Policy on Germany," *Documents on Germany Under Occupation, 1945–1954,* Von Oppen, Beate Ruhm, ed. (London, 1955), pp. 152–160.

American decision at the war's end to halt Lend-Lease had put Britain in what Minister Attlee called "a very serious financial position" because the nation was in no position to begin earning the dollars and gold necessary to pay for imports of food and raw materials. Furthermore, the decision aroused suspicions within the Labor Government that the United States was out to cripple both the Socialist experiment and Britain's economic position in the world. To offset this the American Administration promptly agreed to seek from the Congress a multibillion dollar loan. John Maynard Keynes, the British economist who negotiated the loan in the winter of 1945–1946, knew that America had a stake in a stable free economy; at the same time the American negotiators held out for progressive removal of discriminatory barriers to international trade and free currency convertibility. The passage of the loan was marked by acrimonious attacks by Anglophobes in America and by left-wing elements in the Labor Party, who accused their own government of "subservience to American imperialism" and of being "dragged at the heels of American big business." Nevertheless its passage marked a significant advance in America's march to economic leadership of the non-Communist world. It consolidated a world economy in which the United States' dollar would be the principal trading and banking medium and with it the United States would inherit the miseries and grandeurs so long held by Britain as banker to the world.

Unfortunately, the economic burdens facing Britain "led to a rate of withdrawal of the moneys provided by the American loan at a much greater rate than had been anticipated."[15] As a result, when Britain began to allow its creditors to freely convert their sterling holdings into dollars and gold, the demand was so great that Britain was threatened with exhaustion of its vital stock of dollars and gold to the point of bankruptcy. The experiment in free convertibility lasted six weeks, just long enough to show the bleak and almost hopeless task Britain faced in its economic recovery. Britain and France exhausted the bulk of their loans within six months and Britain was finding herself increasingly unable to perform the imperial tasks that she had previously discharged from Gibraltar to Singapore. Keynes had warned the Labor Government when he negotiated the loan that Britain could no longer afford to maintain her far-flung garrisons. The difficulty of mastering incipient rebellion in Greece, Palestine, India, and Malaya was proving insuperable.

[15] Watt, D. C., "American Aid to Britain and the Problem of Socialism," in *The American Review*, Vol. II, No. 4, March 1963, p. 58.

It became clear as 1946 wore on that the United States could not preserve the world balance of power that it now recognized to be threatened unless it intervened actively and directly to prevent the piecemeal loss of indispensable positions. The United Nations Organization in which Americans had placed so much trust and confidence for the peaceful resolution of disputes was increasingly paralyzed by the Soviet-Western conflict. Action was needed in certain areas which was either not within the competence of the United Nations or which would be paralyzed by a Soviet veto. One of these areas was Greece where the Communist resistance forces had resorted to civil war.

The critical decision was the so-called Truman Doctrine, stated in a message to Congress March 12, 1947. The United States declared its determination to supplant Britain as the guarantor of the Greek government and to employ American funds and military advisers to defeat the efforts of Communist guerrillas to overthrow that government. This policy was a radical departure from the methods that the United States had previously employed to contain the Soviet Union.

The Marshall Plan

But Greece was only a peripheral part of the main theatre, which was the whole of Western Europe. Winter ravages had wiped out whatever gains had been made in the previous year. As long as Europe slowly declined without hope of ultimate recovery, the Soviet Union could afford to bide its time. Sooner or later chaos would ensue and the strong Communist parties of France and Italy would open the way to Soviet domination. Therefore, the plan to extend massive economic aid to Europe—worked out in the State Department in the spring of 1947, stated by Secretary of State George C. Marshall in a Harvard speech on June 5, 1947, seized upon by the French and British governments that summer, and put into operation the following year—represented a far greater setback to Soviet ambitions than the Truman Doctrine. By salvaging Europe and actively recommitting itself to Europe's survival, the United States not only deprived the Soviets of possible victory but suddenly confronted them with the prospect of Western Europe harnessed to a powerful and dangerous capitalist America. Western Europe had not only recovered its economic power in time to stop the spread of Communism, but had also found a powerful ally.

The uncertainty with which the Soviet Union reacted to the American offer of an all-European recovery program is itself indicative of the confusion in the Kremlin. The Soviet Union first agreed to participate in a conference of all European nations which was convened in Paris on June 27, 1947. Molotov headed the Soviet delegation and participated for a few days. Suddenly on June 29, Moscow issued a statement criticizing the British and French proposals. The Soviet attack was essentially directed at the fact that Western proposals seemingly entailed an all-encompassing program to integrate the various national economies. The Soviet statement did not attempt to hide the belief that Marshall Plan aid was likely to be used to promote the economic, and hence the political, expansion of American influence. Molotov's suspicions on this point "were accentuated when he learned that Marshall Aid was not to be administered through any machinery set up by the United Nations but through an independent medium, in which—he assumed—American influence would be unchallenged."[16] On July 2, Molotov quit the conference and a week later the Czechoslovak government withdrew its acceptance.

Moscow had every reason to be disturbed by the implications of the Marshall Plan. The scope and seriousness of the Administration's campaign to win support for the Plan signified the unusual importance attached to its success. Hitherto the Administration had depended largely upon its political resources to secure approval for its plans. Now it enlisted the almost messianic zeal of the biggest financial and industrial interests: Bernard Baruch, Paul Hoffman (Studebaker), Philip Reed (General Electric), John McCloy (Chase National Bank), R. W. Gifford (Borg-Warner), and others. The reception given the Marshall Plan by these titans of industry marked an important evolution in American foreign policy. The isolationists like Robert Taft and Herbert Hoover and extreme laissez-faire opponents of foreign "give-aways" were hopelessly outnumbered. Furthermore the Plan stirred American generosity and its popularity displaced for a time the hysterical anti-Communism associated with the later McCarthy era. Americans felt compensated for a time for the unwelcome intrusion of foreign affairs into their private existence.

Marshall's proposal of a coordinated program of economic assistance was especially congenial to the American style. "Traditionally,

[16] Ingram, Kenneth, *History of the Cold War* (London: Finlayson, 1955), p. 61.

Americans have lacked the inhibitions about involvement in international commerce that they have felt about involvement in international power politics."[17] But more than that: "Achievement in this [economic] sphere of the nation's life has historically been so stupendous and has mitigated so many other kinds of problems that Americans have naturally been inclined to seek for economic solutions to manifold tensions at home and abroad, often with grossly exaggerated hopes for the social and political efficacy of some particular set of economic arrangements."[18] Americans have found it easier to reconcile their moral scruples with the exercise of economic power than with the practice of power politics. And finally, the Marshall Plan received a brilliant reception because "the skills, institutions, contacts, and outward orientation many Americans formed while participating in the network of private and semi-public economic relationships"[19] were potentially more compatible with foreign policy strategies of an economic character than with strategies of a diplomatic, cultural, or military sort.

Within Europe, the Marshall Plan meant not only the end to any hopes the Kremlin might have entertained that Communism might still triumph through chaos in Western Europe, but it also meant that the West would now begin to challenge Soviet hegemony in Eastern Europe. Andrei Y. Vyshinsky, the Soviet delegate to the United Nations, expressed the general Soviet attitude when he declared:

> As is now clear, the Marshall Plan constitutes in essence merely a variant of the Truman Doctrine adapted to the conditions of post-war Europe. In bringing forward this plan, the United States Government apparently counted on the cooperation of the Governments of the United Kingdom and France to confront the European countries . . . with the necessity of renouncing their inalienable right to dispose of their resources [and] on making all these countries directly dependent on the interests of American monopolies. . . .[20]

Soviet leaders were particularly conscious of the implications that the Marshall Plan might have for Germany. Economic, political, strategic, and technological power factors all coalesce in the struggle over Germany because neither Eastern nor Western Europe can be

[17] Westerfield, B., *The Instruments of America's Foreign Policy* (New York: Crowell, 1963), p. 263.

[18] *Ibid.*, p. 264.

[19] *Ibid.*

[20] Vyshinsky, Andrei, "Speech to the U.N. General Assembly (September 18, 1947)," *Official Records*, Plenary Session, Verbatim Record. September 18, 1947, pp. 86–88.

stabilized without Germany. Not only is Germany a prize in itself, but as many scholars have pointed out, "the unchallenged position of the Soviet Union in Eastern Europe cannot be permanently assured as long as Germany with its reservoir of skilled manpower, scientific tradition, and industrial strength remains a potential opponent."[21] It is not surprising, therefore, that Vyshinsky dwelled upon the implications for Germany of the Marshall Plan.

> An important feature of this Plan is the attempt to confront the countries of Eastern Europe with a bloc of Western European States including Western Germany. The intention is to make use of Western Germany and German heavy industry (the Ruhr) as one of the most important economic bases for American expansion in Europe, in disregard of the national interests of the countries which suffered from German aggression.[22]

So direct and portentous a challenge to Soviet policy could not help but elicit a powerful response from the Soviet side. It is perfectly clear from this extreme reaction that the masters of the Kremlin regarded the Marshall Plan as the most serious challenge to their plans they had yet faced. In rivalries like the one developing between the United States and the Soviet Union, any significant action taken by one side appears to have threatening implications for the other. The bipolarity of power, that is, the division of power between two rivals, each entirely dependent on its own resources for nerve and power, makes each move seem desperately important. The United States was more and more likely to become oppressed by the never-ending struggle to uphold an unaccustomed political role; the desperate state of the Soviet leadership was soon to be revealed by sweeping measures taken under Stalin and Zhdanov to fuse the Communist empire into a bloc monolithic in thought, spirit, and subservience to Moscow's every wish.

Soviet leaders made no attempt to mask the seriousness with which they viewed the transfusion of American economic and political power into Europe. Capitalism was now declared to have reassumed its imperialist nature. Any illusions that the Communist world might enjoy a respite from struggle and perhaps an easy conquest of power were now shattered. As long as conditions in Western Europe remained unstable, there was little likelihood of any Western interference with the Stalinization of Eastern Europe. The stagnation of Western Germany was particularly important for the

[21] Rubinstein, Alvin, *The Foreign Policy of the Soviet Union* (New York: Random House, 1960), p. 209.
[22] Vyshinsky, *op. cit.*, p. 88.

success of the Soviet enterprise; the position of the Soviet Union in Eastern Europe might be challenged if Germany, with its reservoir of skilled manpower, scientific tradition, and industrial development, were to regain its previous strength. Soviet leaders made no pretense that they were not acutely concerned by the implications which the Marshall Plan would have upon the future of Germany.[23]

The Marshall Plan symbolized the utter dependency of Europe on the United States. Europe now looked exclusively to the United States for hope and initiative. Few Europeans cared to deny that if their civilization was ever to regain its former vitality and distinction, it would be almost entirely because of the United States. It was precisely America's determination to revive Europe from exhaustion and despair that prompted a profound shift in Soviet assumptions.

The Marshall Plan, Zhdanov informed the Party faithful, was to be viewed as the inevitable product of the need of American capitalists to acquire new markets for their products lest they fail to produce the necessary profits. With the Marshall Plan "the United States proclaimed a new frankly predatory and expansionist course. . . .[24]

No one, least of all a Communist, could doubt that once the threat from American sponsorship of the Marshall Plan was stated in such classically hostile terms, Soviet actions would be equally drastic. In the same address, Zhdanov called for the establishment of monolithic unity within the Communist bloc and the regrouping of world Communist parties under a single head—the Cominform. Everywhere in the Eastern zone, Russian control tightened. The liquidation from the East European scene of all elements even remotely hostile to Soviet interests culminated with the overthrow of the non-Communist government of Czechoslovakia (February 1948), which was the last Eastern European outpost to disappear behind the Iron Curtain.

In a classic expression of the dialectic of insecurity, the fall of Prague had far-reaching consequences in the West. "More than any other single Soviet-inspired move, it dispelled remaining Western illusions concerning Soviet intentions, it heightened anxiety over the Soviet threat, and hastened Western rearmament."[25]

The shock to Americans who were not accustomed to seeing governments fall so unexpectedly was even more profound—psycho-

[23] *Ibid.*

[24] Zhdanov, Andrei, *The International Situation* (Moscow: Foreign Publishing House, 1947), p. 33.

[25] Rubinstein, *op. cit.*, p. 242.

logically and politically, if not militarily. Relations between East and West steadily worsened and the Eastern bloc became little more in Western minds than a terrible, inhuman expression of Stalin's monstrous tyranny.

But the worst was not over. On June 8, 1948, the Soviet government, in a calculated bid to thwart the creation of a West German Government and a stable currency for West Germany, imposed a blockade on the Western sectors of Berlin. The Soviet purpose was clear—to evict the Western powers from Berlin—but they lacked the resolution to intercept allied planes flying through the air corridors linking Berlin with West Germany. Once the allied airlift proved able to supply the beleagured city, the Soviets found themselves committed to a lengthy test of strength.

June 1948 also witnessed another historic event that intensified the Cold War. Rather than submit Yugoslavia to the domination of Moscow and the almost certain loss of his own position, Tito broke away from the Soviet bloc and resisted all pressures to capitulate. The world Communist movement had its first "schismatic" and the American government moved swiftly to give support. By the end of 1948, Yugoslavia was receiving both economic and military assistance from Washington.

The fall of Czechoslovakia and the Berlin blockade had repercussions in Western Europe and in Washington. But if Stalin had hoped to drive the Western powers out of Berlin in order to complete the consolidation of Eastern Europe and to intimidate Western Europe, he failed rather badly. Less than a month after the Communists took over full control of Czechoslovakia in February 1948, five nations of Western Europe met at Brussels to form the Western European Union. Within five months secret staff talks were begun with the United States on the formation of a military alliance between Europe and America. In the spring of 1948 Congress approved $5.8 billion for foreign aid, of which $4.8 billion was to be used to continue the European Recovery Program for another fifteen months, the balance being earmarked for aid to Nationalist China. Already Europe was making a strong recovery. The Administration also began to consider seriously what type of strategy would best deter a Soviet land move across Western Europe. The Strategic Air Command had grown considerably in 1948 and had begun a crash program to achieve a new intercontinental bomber force. But raw power was not enough.

Instead of Stalin having intimidated Europe, the movement toward the formation of a West German government had spurted ahead.

Similarly in Japan the United States was gradually adopting a policy favorable to the reconstitution of Japan as an important potential ally in a new conflict. Marshall Shulman has summed up the predicament facing Moscow in the spring of 1949.

> . . . it had become evident that the militant phase of Soviet policy set forth in 1946 and 1947 had stimulated a trend heavily adverse to Soviet interests. The Soviet Union was confronted with the estrangement of Yugoslavia, the weakening and isolation of its instruments in France and Italy, and the increasing cohesion and military reinforcement of the powers around American leadership.[26]

Furthermore, Soviet leadership now discovered that the Marshall Plan and the Western armament programs were averting the long-awaited American economic collapse and were producing a temporary stabilization of capitalism.

The North Atlantic Treaty

On the American scene the interaction of domestic and foreign policy had worked to the benefit of the Administration. Truman won an unexpected Presidential victory in 1948, in spite of the defection of the Wallace forces, over the Republican candidate, Thomas Dewey. General Marshall resigned as Secretary of State and was replaced by Dean Acheson. Acheson had a clearer sense of the nature of Soviet strategy than either of his postwar predecessors and a more fixed notion of how it could best be met.

From the outset Acheson was determined not to seek compromise for its own sake. He placed very little if any faith in the ability of negotiations and agreements to produce a durable relationship with the Soviet Union. He believed that the Soviets recognized only facts and that they would respect only Western positions based upon military and political strength. Furthermore, Acheson believed that a workable American deterrence to Soviet seizure of Western Europe depended upon the emplacement of American ground forces and the American strategic bomber wings as close to the Soviet industrial heartland as strategy would permit. Hence Acheson determined to push ahead with the North Atlantic Treaty and with the buildup of Western military strength. The European dependency upon the United States facilitated this new American strategy. The North Atlantic Treaty, America's first peacetime alliance was signed April 4,

[26] Shulman, Marshall, *Stalin's Foreign Policy Reappraised* (Cambridge, Mass.: Harvard University Press, 1963), pp. 29–30.

1949. It obliged the signatories to take up arms immediately against an armed attack threatening the security of any member.

The creation of the North Atlantic Treaty and the establishment of a coordinated military force in Europe did not make the conduct or resolution of the Cold War any easier. Both sides were becoming engaged in an out-and-out power struggle, in which subversion on one side was met by a call for a crusade on the other.

The stunning rapidity with which the Soviets saw their advantages reversed in Western Europe and the unexpectedly rapid revival of West Germany and Japan and their shift from passivity to active adherence of the American bloc caught the Soviets by surprise. This adverse shift in the balance of power was offset for the Soviet Union, however, by the successful achievement and detonation of an atomic bomb and by the victory of the Chinese communists on the mainland of China.

Victory of Chinese Communism

The destiny of China had been in the balance for many decades. In China, as elsewhere in Asia, the war had undermined the last foundations of the old order. Despite the Open Door and other expressions of American interest in China, the United States had never been able to decide whether its concern was based on national interest or merely on sentiment. In the absence of any clear conception, neither the Administration nor the American people could decide whether to exert America's power in China or withdraw. Prompted by traditional reluctance to become involved in another nation's civil war and by disgust with Chiang Kai-shek's inept regime, the Administration never felt able to support the Nationalist regime unreservedly. It assumed that neither the Congress nor the American people would support the kind of sacrifices that effective measures would require and thereby "precluded a full exploration of those measures and in effect killed any possibility of discovering that the assumption might be wrong."[27]

During the postwar interregnum the Soviet Union sought to protect its security without committing itself completely to either the Nationalists or the native Chinese Communist movement under Mao Tse-tung. While preserving outwardly "correct" diplomatic relations

[27] Hilsman, Roger, "Congressional-Executive Relations and the Foreign Policy Consensus," *American Political Science Review,* LLI, No. 3 (September, 1958).

with Chiang Kai-shek's regime, Moscow worked for a Communist victory. Because the Nationalist regime was corrupt and ineffective, the Communists were strikingly successful. They soon drove the Nationalists from the mainland and the Chinese People's Republic was proclaimed in Peking on October 1, 1949. Despite some efforts by Stalin to retain a vestige of direct Soviet influence over Chinese territory, even Moscow had to recognize that for the first time in over a century China was controlled by its own Chinese elite "ruthlessly intent on creating a powerful, industrialized, totalitarian China."[28]

Moscow quickly recognized that the new Communist regime had to be treated with far more circumspection than the typical East European satellite. Not only had Mao, like Tito, come to power on his own, but he commanded his own army and ruled over a vast land mass. China could not be controlled as a satellite. Mao journeyed to Moscow in December 1949. Two months later the Chinese delegation took back with them three agreements. The first provided for a military alliance directed against the United States; the second called for a Soviet renunciation by the end of 1952 of all Russian rights in Manchuria except in Darien; the third agreement provided for a $300 million Soviet credit to Peking.

Truman and his principal foreign policy adviser, Secretary of State Acheson, were aware of the adverse and potentially dangerous consequences that might occur should the United States refuse to recognize the transformation wrought by the Communist conquest of power. Acheson was inclined to recognize Red China and not to appear to interfere with mainland China's claim to Formosa (Taiwan). Unfortunately, a century of civil war, unequal treaties, forced concessions to foreign powers, and American support of Chiang Kai-shek had not prepared the Communists to view the United States except with utter hostility. There was no inclination on the part of the new regime to establish normal relations with the United States. Conversely, the shock of the loss of China in addition to the humiliating treatment meted out to United States consular officials combined to produce a violently irrational reaction in America toward the Chinese Communists. The Administration felt politically constrained not to recognize the new government in Peking. Whether the Chinese People's Republic would have reciprocated is a moot question. It is indisputable, however, that the failure to establish normal relations at the time left the United States without

[28] Rubinstein, *op. cit.*, p. 247.

a direct means of communication or intelligence when the Korean War forced us into a direct confrontation.

The loss of China and the Soviet atomic explosion of September 1949 had prompted a reappraisal of American defense policy within the Administration. The extension of Communist control over China made an examination of American policy in Asia absolutely imperative. Together the two events extended the terrain of possible Communist action and lowered the threshold at which the United States might expect Communist military action. The prevailing level of military expenditure barely provided enough military power to cover America's previous strategic commitments. Now with America's nuclear monopoly broken and China lost to Communism, the situation clearly called either for a scaling down of America's objectives or a radical increase in America's strategic capability. An intense debate went on within the Administration, between representatives of the State Department and the Pentagon, during the winter and spring of 1950. These discussions led to recommendations to the President for a considerably expanded military effort that were incorporated in National Security Paper No. 68. The architects of NSC 68, including President Truman, knew that it would be difficult to persuade the American people to accept the tax increases connected with a higher level of defense spending. Republicans like Robert Taft found an attentive audience for their argument that America's greatest strength lay in its free economy and that "additional" taxes would shackle and discourage economic incentive. They even argued that the Communists were intent upon tricking the United States into unduly heavy foreign policy spending as a means of destroying the American economy. Truman, who basically favored a balanced budget himself, found it difficult to meet this argument, which had an undeniable appeal. The success of America's free-enterprise economy would somehow produce the answer to the challenge of Communism. If war came, the United States would win it as it had won past wars by all-out mobilization of its resources. But until then it was best not to overburden the economy with additional taxes and defense expenditures. Of course this did not answer the question of how to maintain national security without a war.

The disturbing imbalance of American strategy—an almost total reliance upon A-Bombs and the Strategic Air Command—was also at the root of an impassioned debate among the nuclear scientists, the Atomic Energy Commission, the Pentagon, and the policy planners in the Department of State. Here too the decision of February 1950 to proceed with the H-Bomb was made without a decision about how to achieve an overall strategic balance. True, plans were going ahead for the establishment of a unified NATO Command with the intention of creating a military force sufficient to defend Western Europe against Soviet attack long enough for America's nuclear strike force to demolish the Russian homeland. Some United States Army planners charged with working out plans for the defense of Europe and some State Department officials, such as Dean Acheson and Paul Nitze, keenly appreciated the strength that would accrue to such a defense from a strong rearmed West Germany. Such a force would relieve the United States of some of the defense burden, but other countries, especially France, could hardly be expected to look with equanimity on German rearmament. The Europeans were still too weak to do much for themselves and the American people, especially Congress, were unwilling to make a major contribution until they had proof that the Europeans were doing their part. Acheson tried to rally American opinion during the spring of 1950 to meet the new demands of American security with calls for "total diplomacy" and "situations of strength." But until something drastic happened Americans preferred to not think about the added costs of world leadership.

Korean Conflict

Nowhere was the American plight more uncertain than in the Far East, where the dust was beginning to settle after the fall of China. A peace treaty was being considered for Japan that would have the effect of ending the occupation and thereby capitalizing upon Japanese friendship. Elsewhere in Asia the Administration had adopted a policy of support for all nationalist movements—as in Indonesia—in the belief that nationalism offered the best bulwark against Communism. It was an article of faith within the State Department that sooner or later the Chinese Communists would have to choose between subservience to Soviet domination and the aspirations of their own people and that the United States should do nothing to deflect Chinese wrath away from this Moscow-centered imperialism. As part of this policy, President Truman had endorsed the State Department's position that the United States should pursue a hands-off attitude regarding Formosa over bitter protests by the "Asia-first" wing of the Republican Party.

Because of the continuing severe limitations upon American military power and the rather formalistic way in which strategic dispositions were made regarding the Far East, South Korea appeared to have been written off as a strategically vital entity. Acheson failed to include South Korea within America's defense perimeter in an important address of January 12, 1950, and later that spring the House defeated the Korean Aid Bill. The deeper explanation for the North Korean aggression in June 1950 must be found in the Communist injunction "to fill up every nook and cranny in the world basin of power" and in the light of America's obvious intention of restoring Japan to power.

It took the actual fact of North Korean aggression to demonstrate just how interrelated and compelling America's worldwide responsibilities had become. In the week following the North Korean attack, the United States committed its forces to the defense of a country whose terrain had previously been considered strategically expendable. Why? The Korean aggression was immediately interpreted in the light of Britain's experience at Munich. Dictators' appetites grow with eating and if allowed to get away with one aggression, they will be encouraged to perpetrate another. The integrity of America's pledge to defend its European allies would be judged by the resolution with which it acted to stem aggression in Korea. And it was felt that the strategical balance already shaken by the loss of China would be irretrievably upset should the United States fail to respond. Ill-prepared though the country might be, the Administration quickly determined that it had no choice but to intervene.

The initial success of America's intervention under the aegis of the United Nations and MacArthur's brilliant blow at Inchon lured the Administration into attempting to unify all of Korea by destroying the North Korean Army and advancing to the Yalu River. This decision is an interesting example of the tendency of national leaders to compartmentalize their thinking, pursuing a course of action that in another sense they know to be treacherous. From the onset of the war American decision-makers had been haunted by the possibility that the aggression in Korea might be only a diversionary attack aimed at consuming what limited military resources America possessed in a hopeless war on the Asian mainland while Russia remained free to advance into an undefended Western Europe. And yet the Administration leaders conceived the notion that the United Nations Command might unite all of Korea in spite of repeated Chinese Communist warnings that such an effort would be met with force.

The decision of whether to take these Chinese threats seriously was in effect left to the commander in the field. He was told that if he encountered heavy forces of Chinese he should disengage; but what if the confrontation took a form from which one could not easily disengage? General MacArthur was a brilliant strategist, noted for his insubordination to his civilian and military superiors and for a tendency to indulge a fatal streak of military romanticism, which in this case led him to view himself as ordained to carry on the nineteenth-century American mission of guarding the Orient for a higher destiny.

Basically American society was once again indulging in the fatal game of underestimating the Oriental. We had done it with the Japanese and suffered Pearl Harbor. Now an Administration that had every reason possible to want to avoid war with China chose to ignore repeated Chinese warnings of intent and to underestimate the improvement that Communist leadership had wrought in the fighting ability of the Chinese soldiers. The propensity to underestimate the Chinese Communist intent and capability was linked with a deprecation of the integrity of Indian Ambassador Pannikkar and with an overestimate of the willingness of the Soviet Union to risk a major conflict. In fact, American intelligence followed a curious pattern all through the war in Korea. When the aggression first occurred, United States intelligence claimed the Soviet bloc was ready for war everywhere; but after Inchon, intelligence was lulled into a fatal underestimation of Chinese propensity to intervene; then when the blow fell, intelligence raised the estimate of the total Communist threat. The obvious implications of such an advance to a strategically critical frontier of a powerful state dedicated to America's defeat was completely discounted until General MacArthur's armies were committed; then it was too late.

Although America's European allies had endorsed the policy of seeking to unify Korea by military means (United Nations Resolution of October 7, 1950), they were shocked when, following the Chinese intervention, President Truman, in response to questions in a press conference on November 30, indicated that the United States might use the atomic bomb. This statement aroused such a storm in the House of Commons that Prime Minister Attlee flew to the United States to seek Truman's assurance that the bomb would not be used.

The outbreak of the Korean War had forced the United States to increase military appropriations greatly. The defeat of United Nations forces and the ensuing struggle with Red China reinforced the United States' propensity toward a much greater level of military preparedness and toward acceptance of the prospect of a military showdown with the Communist bloc. Only the reluctance of the principal governments on both sides to become involved in a third world war, which is what would probably have developed, kept hostilities limited to the Korean peninsula.[29] Neither side achieved the total victory it had looked for. The United States might have taken a greater risk and utilized its air and naval power to force China to negotiate an armistice more quickly. That it did not do so is in itself important evidence of a degree of restraint.

The historical importance of the Korean conflict is therefore twofold: it signified America's willingness to go to war to defend its allies and its strategic interests, and it substituted limited war for total war as a test of relative strength and will. Whether Korea represented just another chapter in the chain wars of the twentieth century or a trend away from total war as a "solution" to international tension and conflict is still to be seen.

The intensity of American reaction to events in Korea eventually led to a "militarization" of containment that was not always the most effective way of dealing with the complex political strategy favored by the Kremlin. The shock that American leadership felt in the face of the Communist bloc's ability and evident willingness to risk a sizeable war prompted a desperate all-out effort to overcome the weaknesses in Western defenses. The United States called upon its allies to join it in a maximum military effort. This appeal in turn put an unduly heavy economic burden upon America's allies, who had not yet fully recovered from the ravages of World War II and whose populations were determined to achieve something of the good life even if it meant taking a risk with their security and survival as free nations. The result of these essentially opposed perspectives—American and European—was an antagonism that was to widen and take many different forms as the 1950's advanced into the 1960's.

Looking back, it does not seem probable that Soviet aggression in Europe should not have been inferred from the North Korean attack. But the Truman Administration seized upon the shock and alarm of the Korean War to push forward its plans for a greatly

[29] Even before Chinese intervention gave the war a much more desperate character, public figures were calling for a showdown. Governor Dewey called war with Russia inevitable (*The New York Times,* September 9, 1950) and an American major general came out in favor of preventive war (*Ibid.,* September 3, 1950). Later on, of course, the pressure got much worse.

increased reservoir of Western power. American military expenditure rose from less than $15 billion to more than $60 billion. The other members of NATO agreed to new military force levels no less ambitious. Sometimes these were set to please the United States and on the assumption that the United States would bail them out if they proved to be beyond European resources. During the first year or two these new defense allocations seemed to place an unduly heavy burden on the European economies in part because they were not fully recovered and in part because an American buying spree in the raw material markets of the world drove up the prices inordinately.

The backlash from the new military budgets struck both the French and British governments especially heavily.

A rift developed in the Labor Party between the Attlee leadership and a faction led by Aneurin Bevan that continued in one form or another for a decade. Aneurin Bevan blamed it all on the United States:

> It is now perfectly clear to anyone who examines the matter objectively that the lurchings of the American economy . . . the failure on the part of the American government to inject the arms programme into the economy slowly, have already caused a vast inflation of prices all over the world, have disturbed the economy of the western world to such an extent that if it goes on more damage will be done by this unrestrained behaviour than by the behaviour of the nation the arms are intended to restrain. . . .[30]

Similar complaints were voiced in France and elsewhere among the NATO allies. In order to meet these complaints, the United States undertook to make several billion dollars available in the form of military aid, loans, and off-shore purchases.

The United States also took advantage of the Korean War to redress the strategic imbalances within the alliance. Some question had always existed in European and American minds about the validity of an alliance that counted upon America's nuclear strike capability both to deter and to defend Europe against a Soviet land thrust. Sooner or later Europeans were bound to question the credibility of America's pledge to defend Europe if it involved the risk of a Soviet nuclear strike at America. The earliest and most lucid response to this query was given by Secretary of State Dean Acheson:

> One reason why we cannot continue to rely on retaliatory airpower as a sufficient deterrent is the effect of time. We have a substantial lead in air power and in atomic weapons. At the present moment, this may be the

[30] Quoted in Rees, David, *Korea: the Limited War* (New York: St. Martin's Press, 1964), p. 239.

most powerful deterrent against aggression. But with the passage of time, even though we continue our advances in this field, the value of our lead diminishes. In other words, the best use we can make of our present retaliatory air power is to move ahead under this protective shield to build the collective balanced forces in Western Europe that will continue to deter aggression after our atomic advantage has been diminished.[31]

On the basis of this strategic rationale, the United States agreed to increase its military assistance to the European allies, to assume the Supreme Command of NATO forces, and to place additional American divisions on the Continent, provided the Europeans accepted a higher level of commitments and contributions and in principle accepted West German participation in the common defense. France proposed that this be achieved through the creation of a European Defense Community which would mobilize and combine German, French, and Benelux forces without actually creating a German army or a German high command.

For a time the panic induced by the Communist aggression in Korea and by the obvious common sense of the strategic rationale for building up NATO produced positive results. The political advantages to the United States of its European alliance were immense. It gave the United States a unique potential for supporting its vital interests through a concert of nations. The ultimate purpose of the alliance was political in the highest sense. But to achieve its maximum political success the alliance had to have a sound coherent strategic and military meaning. Unless the boundary maintenance or security function of the alliance was properly performed, the larger political function of overcoming internal divisiveness and confronting the Soviet Union with the reality of confident strength and a reputation for power combined with restraint and prudence could never have been achieved. It was the great merit of NATO in its early years that it supported the security and diplomacy of the allies against the Soviet bloc and at the same time elicited a high degree of strategic collaboration and political cooperation among the members.

Thus questions that had been unbroachable prior to Korea, such as German rearmament and the level of allied military commitments, were suddenly opened up to discussion and resolution. Within a matter of a few months the American Administration proposed and France accepted, in principle at least, German rearmament.

[31] Acheson, Dean, *Hearings, Assignment of Ground Forces of the United States to Duty in the European Area.* Joint Senate Committee on Foreign Relations and Armed Services. 82 Cong. 1 sess., p. 79.

Eisenhower's appointment as Supreme Commander, the subordination of national armies to a unified mixed command, the creation of the Temporary Council Committee charged with determining the defense expenditures that the respective allies were economically capable of making, and the acceptance of their recommendations, which "obviously exceeded the political, if not the economic, capabilities of the allied governments" constituted a wholly unprecedented degree of abrogation of national authority and integration in time of peace.[32]

In fact, the Soviet Union had begun to adjust its Cold War strategy to take account of America's strong military response to Soviet pressure in Europe and in Korea.[33] Russia's indulgence in open aggression in Korea was the high-water mark of Soviet reliance upon traditional military means. Only after it became apparent that the Korean aggression was not going to succeed and that the American Administration was using Korea to build up its military strength and to mobilize Europe did the Kremlin begin the systematic development of a strategic alternative—the Stockholm peace campaign—followed by the elaboration of "peaceful coexistence." First came the Soviet offer of November 1950 to negotiate a peace treaty for Germany. Then came the encouragement of neutralism, nationalism, the Peace Movement, and anticolonialism. All these means were intended to undermine the American alliance system and divide the Western allies over the already existing divisive issues: economic recovery, the struggle of colonial peoples for independence, and the heavy burden of armaments. Even if the Kremlin had not sought to exploit the stresses imposed upon U. S. diplomacy by the Cold War, the contradictions were sufficiently great to make progress beyond a certain point impossible:

(1) The Europeans had recovered sufficiently to be masters of their own destiny and, once reassured that a Soviet attack upon Western Europe was not imminent, were eager to reap the harvest of economic growth and prosperity.

(2) The acceleration of anticolonial movements that pitted European colonialism against a presumed American sympathy for the peoples seeking independence constituted a growing divisive force in European-American relations. Actually the United States interest in the anticolonial movements was motivated less by anticolonial

[32] Osgood, Robert, *NATO The Entangling Alliance* (Chicago: University of Chicago Press, 1961), p. 82.

[33] Shulman, Marshall, *op. cit.*, p. 258–259.

ideology than by the fear that if they were not recognized they would go Communist. However much common sense there was in the American position, our phobia against Communism sometimes led us into exaggerated and simplified reasoning on this subject and it certainly put the United States deeply at odds with most of its European allies.

(3) Domestically the strains of America's involvement in the Cold War were producing the peculiar fusion of isolationism and chauvinism known as McCarthyism. In fact it was more widespread and deepseated than McCarthyism. Traditional isolationists like Robert Taft had never accepted the notion that America had to assume responsibility for or leadership of the postwar world. Others were frustrated by the Administration's failure to produce miraculous solutions, and still others decried the loss of China and found a convenient rationalization in charges of Communist appeasement. The circumstances under which the Korean War was fought, especially after the intervention of the Chinese Communist armies, fused and reinforced these various strains of dissatisfaction into a boiling cauldron of outrage. At home the duly constituted authorities of government, including (or perhaps especially) the President and the Secretary of State, were under extreme and often irrational attack. Abroad many Americans called for extension of the war to include mainland China, even if it meant "going it alone" and at the risk of all-out war.

Our European allies, not to mention important neutrals like India, were shocked by the threat implicit in talk of preventive war. A widespread contempt for American political life developed among Europeans, alienating even our strongest supporters.

As a result, the moral appeal of American leadership was weakened and the arguments of those who for a variety of reasons were opposed to American policies were strengthened—de Gaullists, neutralists, and Communists in France; Bevanites and "Colonel Blimps" in Britain; Communists, Socialists, and even Catholics in France and Italy.

Conflicts Within NATO

Impressive though they were, NATO and other instruments of American strategy could achieve only limited aims. As soon as it became apparent that the war in Korea was not a prelude to a general war and especially after negotiations began in Panmunjom for a

Korean armistice, the political goals of the members began to take precedence over the collective security and strategic goals of alliance. NATO was after all an alliance and not an organic union. The objectives of the alliance were bound to be defined with reference to the national interest of each of the members and not according to majority rule or some other criterion practiced within the various national communities.

The economic burdens of large-scale rearmament were heavy in every European society. Once the threat of aggression lessened it became more and more difficult to hold the various members to the conditions that they had accepted at the moment of danger. The Pleven Plan (European Defense Community) that France had proposed as a means of controlling German rearmament no longer had the same appeal once it became apparent that France was virtually abrogating its national sovereignty, whereas the United States and Great Britain remained aloof from all supranational associations. West Germany still expected to be compensated for its agreement to align itself with the West. Bonn demanded an end to allied occupation costs and to French control of the Saar, and a Western agreement to give West Germany a virtual veto power over any East-West negotiations involving German interests or a German peace treaty. In short, as its military and security function decreased, NATO began to be used to achieve its members' political objectives, setting up competitive strains within the alliance that were not easily reconcilable.

The most fundamental contradiction within the alliance is the disparity that exists in size and in objectives for NATO between the United States and Europe. For Western Europe, with the single exception of West Germany, NATO is a means of reinforcing the American guarantee of Europe's security. For the United States, NATO is the most likely means to bring pressure upon Communist East Europe. NATO is also the single most important means by which America can hope to subordinate European interests and European energies to the worldwide requirements of America's struggle to contain Communism. A real diplomatic advantage accrues to a power that can control the support and behavior of a dozen or more allies. If they are genuinely concerned for their security and survival as national entities, they will go to considerable lengths to enhance the effectiveness of the alliance. But once the threat to their security is reduced or removed, their willingness to abnegate particularistic interest to the general interest quickly dissipates.

Natural interest soon led the Soviet Union to seek to weaken NATO by exploiting these competing national interests. An armistice in Korea did not end the war but at least reduced the expectation that it might escalate into a general war; new offers to negotiate a peace settlement with Germany gave little promise of a settlement but nevertheless reduced tension there too; finally a vast peace campaign was undertaken to create the impression that the United States and not the Soviet Union was principally responsible for the Cold War. Although few members of Western governments were influenced, these maneuvers reinforced other trends that were running against the American concept of NATO.

America's hopes for NATO were not to be fully realized precisely because NATO succeeded so quickly in becoming what it did. The Soviet Union had to undertake a major shift in its strategy—one that accepted the at least temporary stabilization of capitalism. Any hope of an easy victory over the free world had been rudely shattered. Moreover, NATO represented a solid political and military achievement that Russia would not find easy to overcome. NATO difficulties would stem as much from America's failure to adapt its policies to the changing nature of European political realities as from shifts in Soviet strategy. In the beginning the difference in the relative power and confidence between the United States and Europe allowed a system of informal hierarchy in which Europe could be expected to accept American decisions. But as the European states regained their strength, this hierarchy should have given way to a more equitable system of decision-making. Instead it did not. Moreover, as the threat of direct Soviet military action receded, secondary and tertiary national interests were bound to reassert themselves among the European states. Unfortunately, most Americans lacked sufficient knowledge of international politics to understand how very remarkable an achievement NATO was. To many of them it was not sufficiently dynamic and it gave no promise of yielding immediate victories in the Cold War. Americans simply resented the price they had to pay in terms of involvement and the failure of European states to be more grateful and responsive to American wishes.

Domestic Repercussions of the Cold War

The war in Korea had become a catalyst for many things that Americans found painful and intolerable about the Cold War. The Administration's motives in limiting the war were suspect. The enemy was not being punished to the full extent of America's power. Instead the Administration acquiesced in humiliating defeats and accepted intolerable limitations upon its retaliatory power. Americans were not accustomed to a style of combat that seemed devoid of honor, moral significance, or the satisfying goal of victory. In addition, the Democratic handling of the early Cold War conflict, particularly in Eastern Europe and China, stimulated a sense of guilt about the people lost to Communism. Americans had also grown impatient with the unaccustomed burdens and complexities of international politics.

For years there had been a steady chorus of political and editorial calls for a showdown with Communism. Not since the Great Depression had public attitudes been so aroused.[34]

> There could be no compromise, no half-victory. Advances and losses had to be measured in territory occupied or in the total commitment of other nations to the national interest of the United States. Any deviation from such a principle was to be greeted with confusion. . . .[35]

The frustrations precipitated by the Cold War introduced other symptoms, which in turn fed back to augment the general frustration. As a natural companion to a sense of failure in encounters with the Soviet Union, a disproportionate fear of internal Communism commenced. The power of McCarthyism demonstrated that the public was frantically searching for a simple solution for all its apprehensions. The answer was found in "conspiracy." The Senator's contribution to foreign affairs was to aggravate the moralistic attitude toward the outside world and to distract attention from the true gravity of international problems by his inflation of the specter of internal subversion. McCarthy "offered a refuge in the form of a spiritual tariff barrier from the doubts and indecisions of the outside world."[36]

McCarthyism was a reflection of the general tendency of the American public to explain the course of history after the fact and direct attention away from the complexities of the international scene to the more accessible domestic one. The "sellout" at Yalta invoked visions of subversives high in the administration. The "loss of China" appeared incomprehensible unless colored with the aura of treason. And finally the frustrations of the Korean experience were reinforced

[34] Campbell, Angus, *et al., The American Voter* (New York: John Wiley and Sons, 1960), p. 555.

[35] Goldman, Eric F., *The Crucial Decade and After* (New York: Vintage, 1960), pp. 123–131.

[36] Chandler, Geoffrey, "American Opinion and Foreign Policy," *International Affairs* (London), October 1955, p. 452.

by casualty lists. Messianic, anti-intellectual, and simplistic national characteristics came to the fore; the frustrations preconditioned the public to embrace a new doctrine for winning the Cold War—that of liberation and rollback.

The Republicans had been preparing to capitalize upon this mood of outrage and frustration. The Taft wing of the Party had questioned the wisdom of America forsaking its traditional freedom and security to become embroiled in Europe's problems. Taft's strategy after his 1950 senatorial victory in Ohio had been to exploit the national sense of unease and frustration to condition the country for a return to isolation vis-a-vis Europe and of token involvement in Asia. Another faction within the Republican Party decried containment because it was not sufficiently dynamic and aggressive. Logically they favored more not less involvement.

There were also independents and Republicans such as Walter Lippmann and Emmet John Hughes who believed that American diplomacy needed "freshness of thought" which a re-elected Democratic Administration could not provide, not because of a lack of will, but because any diplomatic ventures would be pitilessly choked off by charges of appeasement. "Only the Republican administration," Hughes asserted, "would have the freedom—the chance—to think anew and act anew."[37]

Beyond ideology the Republican Party confronted the practical issue of whether an isolationist like Taft could be elected. Even though the country was intensely dissatisfied with the Truman-Acheson foreign policy, it was in no mood to revert to isolationism.

It was in this context that the doctrine of liberation was launched and taken up by the Republican Party. The chief complaints against Administration policy were that it was not active or aggressive enough, that its actions were rooted in the immoral assumption that the free world must try to get along with the Communist world, and that it mistakenly believed that if Communist power were merely contained internal contradictions would lead to the blunting of its dynamic force.

Critics of the Administration offered a logically consistent alternative. The Communist world, it was asserted by James Burnham and others, was not a dynamic force challenging a static Western world; in fact, the Soviet system was an artifact that would, with pressure, splinter upon the weak foundations on which it was erected. A

[37] Hughes, Emmet John, *The Ordeal of Power* (New York: Dell, 1963), p. 16.

campaign to liberate Eastern Europe would be one of these pressures, and artfully manipulated, the policy should result in the

> fractionalization of the present Soviet Empire into several dozen wholly independent sovereign and rival states . . . removing the intolerable threat to world security which exists because of the control of all central Eurasia by a single aggressive power apparatus.[38]

Burnham provided the intellectual rationale for the doctrine of liberation and rollback, and the doctrine was given wider substance and authority by John Foster Dulles in May 1952, in *Life* magazine. Dulles was already being prominently mentioned for the post of Secretary of State in any future Republican Administration; therefore his words had the weight not only of a campaign statement but that of a future foreign policy document. The keynote of his proposition was that "our present negative policies will never end the peril nor bring relief from the exertions which devour our economic, political and moral vitals."[39] The Soviet Union must be challenged at those points where it feels secure:

> Courage will not be maintained in the satellites *unless the United States makes it publicly known that it wants and expects liberation to occur.* The mere statement of that wish and expectation would put heavy new burdens on the jailers and create new opportunities for liberation.[40]

A careful reading of Dulles' proposals revealed that little more was outlined than "statements of wishes and aspiration." The political attractiveness of the liberation doctrine lay in its apparent call for bold decisions; it was offered as a positive alternative course of action to that being offered by the Democrats. Above all, it prognosticated results within a definite time-period, the meaning of which was easily understandable and which indicated that freedom's establishment in Eastern Europe—by virtue of Western diplomatic successes —could be achieved within the foreseeable future. Dulles stated:

> Such results will not come to pass overnight. But we can know, as history proves, that the spirit of patriotism burns unquenched . . . and we can be confident that within two, five or ten years substantial parts of the present captive world can peacefully regain their national independence.[41]

38 Burnham, James, *Containment or Liberation?* (New York: John Day Company, 1952), p. 228.
39 Dulles, John Foster, "A Policy of Boldness," *Life* (May 19, 1952), p. 38.
40 *Ibid.*, p. 146.
41 *Ibid.*, p. 153.

Two, five, or ten years: this was a definition that could be comprehended and endorsed. Moreover, a minimum of risk for the United States was entailed, for such goals were to be secured "peacefully." Dulles continued, "We do not want a series of bloody uprisings and reprisals. . . . There can be peaceful separation from Moscow . . . and enslavement can be made so unprofitable that the master will let go his grip."[42]

The appeal of this argument to both the Eisenhower and Taft Republican factions resulted in its integration into the Republican Party platform. Its author, who also wrote the Republican Party's 1952 foreign policy platform, declared that a Republican victory would "mark the end of the negative, futile and immoral policy of 'containment' which abandons countless human beings to a despotism and Godless terrorism which in turn enables the rulers to forge the captives into a weapon for our destruction."[43]

The nomination of General Eisenhower was assurance that the liberation concept would continue as an article of faith by the party leadership committed to parallel internationalism and dynamic action. It corresponded to Eisenhower's personal intellectual beliefs, which in large measure reflected his conviction that the campaign must be conducted as "a great crusade—for freedom in America and freedom in the world." The liberation theme was specifically endorsed by Eisenhower, and continual references were made to it in his speeches:

> We can never rest—and we must so inform all the world, including the Kremlin—that until the enslaved nations of the world have in the fullness of freedom the right to choose their own path, that then, and then only, can we say that there is a possible way for living peacefully and permanently with communism in the world.[44]

Foreign observers interpreted such statements as a commitment by a future Republican administration to view the establishment of free governments in Eastern Europe as a *sine qua non* of peaceful coexistence between the United States and the Soviet Union.[45] An attitude of distrust and uneasiness began to grow in Europe toward the Republican doctrine of liberation. Adlai Stevenson, the Democratic

[42] *Ibid.*, p. 138.

[43] Quoted in Richard P. Stebbins, *The United States in World Affairs 1952* (New York: Harper, 1953), p. 311.

[44] *New York Times,* August 27, 1952, p. 1.

[45] Stebbins, *op. cit.*, p. 311.

candidate, saddled with the record of the Truman Administration, could offer nothing to compare with the popularity of Eisenhower's reputation.

The Republican campaign of 1952 with its emphasis upon the defeat of Communism and its call for liberation and rollback has often been dismissed as meaningless.

> Liberation was the Republican Party's therapy for a public that refused to accept the facts of America's limited power in the world and rejected any changes in its traditional approach to foreign policy. That this policy of liberation was probably never meant to be more than a verbal appeal to the American people was clearly demonstrated at the time of the anti-Communist revolt in East Berlin in June, 1953, and during the national uprising in Hungary in late 1956.[46]

Such generalizations fail to grasp that the liberationist ideology was an expression of dissatisfaction with the progress of the Cold War and an attempt to meet the challenge of Communism on a more profound level. True, "the mere enunciation of the doctrine of liberation would not free any Soviet satellites; good intentions unsupported by concrete political and military policies, possess a notorious impotence on the international scene."[47] Nevertheless the campaign reflected a state of mind into which the Cold War had plunged American opinion and through which it had to pass in order to advance to a more mature realization of its place in history.

American policy would never really depart from its containment posture. Neverthless the attitudes sanctioned by the Republican campaign found expression in many important aspects of American strategy and diplomacy. First, the liberationist ideology masked a nationalism and even an isolationism that was reflected in an attitude that our allies were only important to us because of what they could contribute to our interests and security.

Second, the liberationist ideology reinforced the prevailing tendency in Washington to subordinate all aspects of international policy to the bipolar pattern of the Cold War.

Third, of all the men who came to Washington with the new Administration few better epitomized the ideological and moral fervor of the mandate that the electorate had given Eisenhower than the Secretary of State, John Foster Dulles. When asked a few months before his death whether he saw the struggle with Soviet Communism

[46] Spanier, John, *American Foreign Policy Since World War II* (New York: Praeger, 2nd ed. rev., 1965), p. 106.

[47] Spanier, *ibid.*, p. 105.

primarily as a moral struggle or a power political struggle, Dulles replied: "Primarily as a moral struggle." Dulles had no illusions about the strength and implacability of Communism's determination to rule the world. Because it was a struggle between good and evil, Dulles could not afford to believe that evil might prevail. He tended to believe that inherent weaknesses in the Soviet system would become more pronounced if the West was tough. This exaggerated view sometimes led him to claim that the Communist bloc was on the verge of crumbling. It also gave a very definite cast to his ideas about how relations with the Soviet Union should be conducted. It gave him an incentive to be tough, aggressive, and uncompromising. In a struggle between good and evil there was no place for a defensive posture; "if our policy is stay where we are we will be driven back."

Unfortunately, too much of Dulles' moralism spilled over into his relations with the non-Communist countries. Since Dulles never doubted that America was pursuing a course of righteousness he was quick to assume that America's interests and those of all other non-Communist nations must naturally be harmonious and that any demand America made upon them was not for itself but for a higher cause. This attitude put a heavy burden on America's relations with its allies and with the nonaligned powers who preferred not to choose sides at all.

The effort to create the impression of innovation and at the same time to keep within the limits of fiscal responsibility imposed a tremendous burden upon the new Administration and upon Dulles in particular. The Administration met the challenge by a combination of symbolic acts such as "unleashing" Chiang Kai-shek and by adjustments in American strategy and foreign policy.

CHAPTER 2

The Deadlock of Bipolarity

IN VIEW of the central role that military power plays in the Cold War, an analysis of the Eisenhower Administration's initiatives in strategic doctrine is of great importance. The Administration felt a strong urge to innovate—in part out of dissatisfaction with the previous Administration's handling of the Korean War and in part out of a determination to reduce military spending because it feared excessive governmental spending. This process gave birth to two concepts with which the Administration became indelibly associated and which had an important bearing on the Cold War: the New Look and massive retaliation.

In terms of forces or preparedness policy "the newness of the New Look . . . lay chiefly in reduction of Army and Navy manpower and the increased effort in air defense. In terms of 'action policy'—intentions regarding the use of forces—the change was somewhat sharper. The New Look included a determination to rely more upon nuclear weapons, especially nuclear air power," than had previously been planned.[1] Traditionally the full array of a nation's military power served as both a warning—deterrence—against potential aggression and as the means of defense should aggression occur. The advent of nuclear weapons had changed tradition. Because it was too horrible to contemplate the use of atomic bombs except in defense of the most vital interests, nations would rely primarily upon conventional weaponry for defense. There still remained the enormous expense of maintaining a nuclear capability as an ultimate warning against acts of aggression. At the same time the realization that a nation might have to fight a subnuclear war required the maintenance of a large conventional military establishment. Maintaining two military establishments—one for conventional wars and one for nuclear wars—involved enormous expense and implied that the nation would continue to accept the possibility of fighting in limited conflicts such as in Korea. In an effort to reduce these costs and to reduce the likelihood that the United States would ever again have to fight such a war, the Eisenhower Administration determined to place

[1] Snyder, Glenn, "The 'New Look' of 1953" in *Strategy, Politics and Defense Budgets* edited by Schilling, Warner R., *et al.* (New York: Columbia University Press, 1962), p. 492.

greater reliance upon the nuclear establishment both to deter and to defend against aggression. This determination found expression in a new military doctrine to which Dulles gave the term "massive retaliation."

So long as our basic policy concepts were unclear, our military leaders could not be selective in building our military power. If an enemy could pick his time and place and method of warfare—and if our policy was to remain the traditional one of meeting aggression by direct and local opposition—then we needed to be ready to fight in the Arctic and in the Tropics; and in Asia, the Near East, and in Europe, by sea, by land, and by air; with old weapons and with new weapons. . . . This could not be continued for long without grave budgetary, economic, and social consequences. . . . The basic decision (has been taken) to depend primarily upon a great capacity to retaliate, instantly, by means and at places of our own choosing. Now [we] can shape our military establishment to fit what is our policy, instead of having to try to be ready to meet the enemy's many choices. That permits of a selection of military means instead of a multiplication of means. As a result, it is now possible to get, and share, more basic security at less cost.[2]

Dulles subsequently emphasized that nuclear retaliation was still to be viewed as a potential reinforcement to the first line of defense sustained by NATO and America's allies and he backtracked considerably from his original statement. But as Bernard Brodie says, "if one examines the course actually pursued by national defense policy and military programming over the next several years, it was the original speech which stood and not the retractions."

In a sense the New Look and massive retaliation were not as radical innovations as the Administration sometimes claimed. The death of Stalin, the end of the Korean War, and the softening of the Soviet foreign policy line "would have stimulated considerable popular pressure for retrenchment" under any circumstances.[3] This retrenchment in turn would have produced pressure for reduction in *overall* forces "for the long haul" with a consequent heightening of emphasis upon the air power-deterrence function.

Yet, the New Look cannot be explained entirely as a natural response to external and technological change. The new leadership brought to bear on the defense problem certain special attitudes which made the shift in strategy and forces somewhat sharper than is likely to have occurred as a result of environmental factors alone.[4]

[2] Dulles, John Foster, Address before the Council on Foreign Relations, January 12, 1954. Reproduced in *The New York Times,* January 13, 1954.

[3] Snyder, *op. cit.,* p. 494.

[4] *Ibid.,* p. 495.

Among these Snyder cites "the commitment to a balanced budget at reduced tax rates." But he also cites two other considerations that had a profound effect on all aspects of American foreign relations during the 1950's. Americans sought in military power a sovereign remedy to the nagging political problems posed by the Communist strategic challenge.

From this stemmed an impatience with the concept of limited war, with the idea that the enemy might refrain from using his most powerful weapons if we did likewise. In the context of this attitude, it was simply nonsense not to throw out "outmoded" weapons and strategies and incorporate the newest and most powerful weapons, changing strategy (meaning grand strategy and political strategy) to allow the use of those weapons in the most efficient way. This attitude tended to focus attention on the means of policy—specifically on the maximization of fire power—and to divert attention away from policy ends.[5]

This obsession with military fire power almost to the exclusion of considerations of military and political ends, had detrimental consequences for United States policy. It fed the "pactomania" and reduced NATO considerations to exercises in weaponry.

The New Look also revealed the same self-centeredness in the Administration's strategic thought as in its diplomacy.

The Truman Administration had taken seriously the dictum that in alliance diplomacy the interests of the members must be fostered at all times; the interests of one's allies and those whom one wishes to influence must be made one's own; an effort must always be expended to maintain or renew a sufficient identity or mutuality of interest to sustain the burden of common engagement in a difficult enterprise.

The New Look reflected a different attitude, a subtle form of isolationism. By "upgrading" nuclear airpower to the position of the decisive instrument of *defense* in case the enemy was not deterred and by providing for the "disengagement" of American forces from distant theaters and their redeployment in a "central strategic reserve," the Administration was actually attempting to throw a greater burden upon the allies and at the same time to reduce America's level of involvement. In a sense this same attitude lay behind Dulles' threat of "agonizing reappraisal" should France not ratify EDC and the Administration's efforts to substitute tactical nuclear weapons for manpower.

It was characteristic of the outlook behind these policies that no aspect of the New Look decisions "was cleared or discussed to any

[5] *Ibid.*

significant degree with the other NATO allies until after the decisions had been taken."

Obviously had war come the United States would have paid for the onesidedness of its strategic dispositions. Fortunately war did not come and it is even possible to argue that the New Look was a calculated risk worth taking. As David Abshire puts it, "The success of the Eisenhower-Dulles strategy of securing maximum deterrence value from our margin of superiority compensated for a potential lack of versatility on lower levels of conflict."[6]

This position makes a virtue out of a fault. Sooner or later the limitations of the New Look philosophy and doctrine were bound to show up, in Europe in the loss of confidence in the credibility and in the strategic rationale of NATO; elsewhere in the gap between the Administration's determination not to yield an additional inch of territory to the Communist bloc and the rigidity of the means by which it proposed to deter it.

Massive retaliation required that definite lines be drawn to make clear in advance to the enemy that his aggression would trigger a massive response by the United States. This belief led the United States into a series of pacts and mutual defense treaties which "were not, except in a minor and subsidiary way, attempts to create military organizations or military strength in the manner of NATO: they were so many devices for defining the perimeter, "Thin Ice" signs erected for the benefit of observers in Moscow."[7] They, nevertheless, involved an expansion of America's formal commitments and were not always well received by all the governments whose security they were designed to protect. Many governments in the Middle East and Southeast Asia refused to belong to SEATO or the Bagdad Pact. Dulles' efforts to ring the Soviet bloc with pacts of military precision and comprehensiveness was marred by frequent gaps into which Soviet diplomacy probed with devastating efficiency.

The Indochina War and the Geneva Agreements of 1954

The credibility of brinkmanship and of massive retaliation was posed for Dulles by the collapse of the French war in Indochina in 1954. Following the defeat of Chiang Kai-shek and the outbreak of the Korean War, the United States had supplied the French with large

[6] Abshire, David M., "Grand Strategy Reconstructed," *Detente,* edited by E. L. Dulles and R. D. Crane (New York: Praeger, 1965), p. 257.

[7] Bell, Coral, *Negotiation From Strength* (New York: Knopf, 1963), p. 93.

sums of money and equipment to help defeat the Communist-led Viet Minh movement under Ho Chi Minh. The Eisenhower Administration eagerly pursued an armistice in Korea but it preferred to see the French continue their war in Indochina. The French resented being pressured to continue the war in Viet Nam, a war that was becoming increasingly hopeless, which Frenchmen knew Americans regarded as a contemptible colonial war, and to which the French citizens gave less and less support.

Dulles now warned the Chinese Communists that any aggression—open intervention—on behalf of the Viet Minh would incur "grave consequences which might not be confined to Indochina." Dulles next defined the strategic importance that the United States attached to Indochina:

> Under the conditions of today, the imposition on Southeast Asia of the political system of Communist Russia and its Chinese ally, by *whatever* means, would be a grave threat to the whole free community. The United States feels that that possibility should not be passively accepted, but should be met by united action. This might have serious risks, but these risks are far less than would face us in a few years from now if we dare not be resolute today.[8]

But when it came to actually making good on this threat not to accept passively a Communist-style regime in Indochina other considerations prevailed. It is certainly true that the Administration did not care to be associated openly with the French in a colonialist war. But more important, neither the President nor the American Congress nor the Army Chief of Staff were willing to become involved in another land war on the Asian mainland. As a result the massive retaliation doctrine was not put to the test. The Administration did not believe that dropping atom bombs on Moscow or Peiping or any other point of America's choosing on the Communist side of the Iron Curtain was worth the political consequences. It was made abundantly clear even then that without the willingness and capability to fight a limited war, the threat of massive retaliation was less than useless to defeat limited transgressions.

For some time Soviets had been attempting to halt the war in Indochina. Soviet Foreign Minister Molotov had suggested to his French counterpart, Georges Bidault, that the Soviet Union would arrange an armistice in Indochina in exchange for French abandonment of EDC. With American talk of intervening Soviet efforts took

[8] Quoted in Spanier, John W., *American Foreign Policy* (New York: Praeger, 1962), p. 109.

on added urgency. Should America expand hostilities, China was likely to become involved; the Soviets were bound by the Sino-Soviet alliance of 1950 to go to China's assistance in such a contingency. The new Soviet leaders were especially anxious to avoid nuclear war, but neither Communist state had an interest in becoming engaged in a general war at a time when the nuclear balance still heavily favored the United States. Ho Chi Minh was accordingly persuaded to settle for limited victory and only the northern half of Viet Nam.

At the same meetings at which massive retaliation and air strikes in support of the beleagured French garrison at Dien Bien Phu were ruled out, Administration leaders agreed that if America could obtain some form of effective collaboration from its allies, notably Britain, it would commit the United States to some form of military support for the French. Dulles flew to London where Eden gave the treaty proposal a hearing. Dulles returned to Washington believing that he had had a favorable reaction to ideas that took the form of the Southeast Asia Collective Defense treaty, signed in September 1954. But upon deliberation Eden refused to join the United States in supporting the French in Indochina. Eden preferred not to widen the war just when the combatants were meeting at Geneva to negotiate an acceptable settlement. He also distrusted Dulles' intentions. Dulles never forgave Eden for letting him down. It was never easy for Dulles to accept personal defeat in his diplomacy and he tended to put the blame on others in matters for which he was equally responsible. Dulles now nurtured a grievance against Eden that would weaken their relationship and have tragic implications at the time of the Suez Crisis.[9]

Unable to secure American assistance, the French Government decided to make the best of the situation by negotiating an end to the war. Dulles, for a variety of reasons, refused to participate in the Geneva negotiations in the summer of 1954. (He attended for a week, departing on May 3, never to return, but he finally agreed to let Under-Secretary of State Bedell Smith attend.) He abhorred the circumstances under which the Conference was taking place and he preferred not to be present at a Communist triumph over the West, especially when it might cause him embarrassment with the wing of his own party mainly concerned with Asia. He was determined not to act in any way that would lead to either recognition of China or Peiping's entry into the United Nations. Dulles also wanted to make

[9] Goold-Adams, Richard, *The Time of Power: A Reappraisal of John Foster Dulles* (London: Weidenfeld and Nicolson, 1962), p. 135.

it clear to Peiping and Moscow that America did not approve of the agreement and did not want the Communists to assume at any time that America had washed its hands of Indochina. Dulles believed that he could make his biggest contribution to the conference by skulking in the background as a warning to Peiping that the United States was ready to pounce upon any terms unacceptable to the French to reopen the whole war. Dulles believed that his absence from the conference warned the Chinese that, however many successes they might achieve, the United States could not tolerate total victory and the fall of Southeast Asia. He had said that he would never put his signature to a document condoning any Communist acquisition of territory. Consequently when on July 20, 1954, the conferees agreed to an armistice dividing Indochina at approximately the 17th parallel and providing for the withdrawal of all troops and bases from the four states of North Viet Nam, South Viet Nam, Laos, and Cambodia and for free elections at the end of two years, the United States did not sign. Instead the United States merely took note of the declaration of agreement and added that it would view any renewal of aggression with grave concern.

The Geneva accords were very much a great-power settlement in that the partition reflected the interplay of Soviet and American national interests; Pham Van Dong, the Viet Minh Foreign Minister, reportedly complained to friends after the Geneva Conference that the elections would never be held.[10] Because South Viet Nam produced most of the country's rice, partition constituted a built-in incentive for the Viet Minh to renew hostilities if the opportunity arose to do so.

In effect the Geneva Agreements terminating the war marked the end of the French phase of the Viet Nam story and the beginning of the American phase. Dulles is reputed to have said that the Geneva Agreements were a blessing in disguise because they removed French influence and allowed the United States to intervene free of the taint of colonialism. According to Dulles' view of Communism, there was never any question about the wisdom of what America next proceeded to do. The United States brushed aside the remaining French influence in South Viet Nam, deposed Bao Dai, and replaced him with Ngo Dinh Diem, and provided Diem with economic and military aid to help stabilize his regime. Dulles had no intention of letting any

[10] Honey, P. J., "North Vietnam's Party Congress," *The China Quarterly* (October–December, 1960).

part of Asia go by default or by free elections to the Communists. The question of whether America could make good on that commitment was left to others to determine.

The South East Asia Treaty Organization

History works in mysterious ways. The circumstances under which the French war in Indochina came to an end brought the United States into Southeast Asia for the first time (except for the Philippines). Perhaps it was inevitable that with the liquidation of the only other form of power in the area—European imperialism—the United States should become involved. Perhaps Dulles overreacted out of an obsession with the danger of Communist expansion. Whatever the explanation the United States took the occasion to extend the line of American defense to the rest of Southeast Asia through the instrument of SEATO. Of the Asian states only Pakistan, Thailand, and the Philippines were signatories of SEATO, although treaty protection extended to Laos, Cambodia, and South Viet Nam. The other Asian states refused to join because they were convinced that joining one side or the other would only implicate them in a quarrel from which it was in their best interest to remain aloof. The fact that neutralism or nonalignment contradicted Dulles' thesis that the Cold War was a moral struggle from which no nation could righteously abstain destroyed much of his effectiveness in dealing politically with the Asians. The United States in turn suddenly found itself implicated in matters such as the Pakistan-Indian dispute over Kashmir in which it had no interest whatsoever. Whether drawing the line by such an artificial means was the best way politically and strategically of meeting the Communist challenge in Asia is debatable. Could not the same ends have been more efficaciously achieved by simple bilateral treaties between the United States and those nations wishing an American guarantee?

After Stalin's Death

In addition to all the other internal contradictions besetting American foreign policy in the years after 1952, Eisenhower and Dulles themselves were divided on foreign policy. Eisenhower cast himself as a man of peace and most initiatives at peace-seeking came from the White House; Dulles was by temperament committed to prosecution of the Cold War at all hazards.[11] Dulles was convinced beyond peradventure or reasoning that nothing good could come from negotiation with the Communists.

The divergent strains within the new Administration were soon put to the test. As long as Stalin was alive, the Soviet peace offensive had lacked ultimate conviction. On March 5, 1953, death came to Stalin. The fall of the Soviet titan was bound to have an impact upon world expectations. In the uncertainty about what the United States response ought to be, Eisenhower gave full expression to his peace philosophy.

In preparing his first speech after Stalin's death, Eisenhower had it purged of "any allusions to 'liberation' of Eastern Europe or 'unleashing' of Nationalist China. . . ."[12] Instead Eisenhower held out to the new men in the Kremlin a conciliatory olive branch:

> We care only for sincerity of peaceful purpose, attested by deed. . . . Even a few such clear and specific acts, such as the Soviet Union's signature upon an Austrian treaty or its release of thousands of prisoners still held from World War II would be impressive signs. . . .
>
> The first great step along this way must be the conclusion of an honorable armistice in Korea.[13]

Stalin's passing had an even greater impact upon European thinking. The new men in the Kremlin wasted no time in sponsoring all manner of tempting and reassuring tokens of good will. The very change in the Soviet tone and posture was so striking as to produce a warm response in various Western quarters. Churchill had been promoting the idea of negotiations ever since the spring of 1950. Now that Stalin was gone, he renewed his plea for a Summit meeting of Soviet and Western leaders.

The apparent successor, Georgi Malenkov, and his colleagues wasted little time in meeting the essential stipulations of Eisenhower's peace offer. The long drawn-out negotiations for a Korean armistice were expeditiously completed (July 1953). Next a peace treaty for Austria, which had been sitting on the shelf, was dusted off and placed on the altar of negotiations. The Austrian State Treaty, providing for the withdrawal of all occupation forces and the acceptance

[11] Hughes, Emmet John, *The Ordeal of Power* (New York: Dell, 1963), pp. 91–92.

[12] *Ibid.*, p. 95.

[13] *The New York Times,* May 19, 1955.

by Austria of a status of permanent neutrality between East and West, was signed on May 15, 1955.

Normal relations were restored with Yugoslavia. The Porkala Naval Base taken from Finland in 1940 was restored to the Finns. These gestures had their effect and prompted speculation as to whether the Soviet line was not changing and softening. The Western allies agreed to a Summit Meeting of the four heads of state: Eisenhower, Eden, Faure, and Bulganin (Khrushchev attended as Secretary of the Soviet Communist Party).

Geneva Conference of 1955

The motives for the conference on the part of the participants are fairly well established. Initially the Soviets had hoped by convening the conference to forestall the arming of West Germany. Following the defeat of EDC and the success of Eden's efforts to bring about German rearmament under the aegis of the Western European Union, the Soviet objective became to delay German reunification. We now know that this objective was reinforced by decisions concerning Soviet global strategy.

> At a Plenum of the Central Committee which opened July 4 and closed six days before the Geneva Conference, the basic Soviet global strategy was revised. The Soviet Union would take the offensive in Asia to detach the underdeveloped countries from capitalism, sealing the fate of the West by the "capture" of India. Meanwhile the strategy of "defense in Europe" must be actively conducted, while avoiding conflict. Certainly any modification of the German problem other than stabilization of the status quo would not have fitted this strategy.[14]

There are precious few junctures in the Cold War to which one can point and wonder if some measure of accommodation might have been possible. Was the Soviet interest in convening a Summit Conference exclusively for purposes of launching a new strategic offensive or was there some potential for a détente, or relaxation of tension, on the model of the subsequent Kennedy détente, that might have been nurtured? There are those who argue that there was absolutely no possibility at the time.

Whether more could have been gained from the conference will never be known because of the divergent motives with which Eisen-

[14] Davis, Raul C., "The New Diplomacy," in *Foreign Policy in the Sixties,* Hilsman, Roger, and Good, Robert C. (eds.), (Baltimore: Johns Hopkins University Press, 1965), p. 163.

hower and Dulles approached it. It is worth noting that each based his approach on the same assumptions of American strength and relative Soviet weakness (East German uprising, economic stringencies within the Communist bloc, and so forth), but each drew a different conclusion. Dulles saw in Soviet weakness a condition to be exploited; Eisenhower saw in the possibility of greater reasonableness on the part of the Kremlin.

There was the second ambivalence—that between the President's urgent desire to create a new spirit and his concern lest its failure injure domestic morale. The quest for a new spirit dominated, however, breaking through the membrane of caution in his public utterances, and appearing in a form more exaggerated even than his private hopes, evidently because of his sense of the dramatic quality of his own destiny. All this is evident, for example, in one sentence . . . "I say to you if we can change the spirit in which these conferences are conducted we will have taken the greatest step toward peace, toward future prosperity and tranquillity that has ever been taken in all the history of mankind." It was his sense of mission as peacemaker which led him also to exaggerate the dangers of war. Other Presidents had gone abroad in their war-conducting or war-settling capacities. "But now," he continued, "for the first time, a President goes to engage in a conference with heads of other governments in order to prevent war. . . ." In the light of such a statement it is interesting to recall that, though the ominous cloud of the H-bomb then floated over the world, there were at the time of Geneva no military crises such as had existed the year before or have dogged the world since the year after.
Dulles, as we have seen, gave reserved support to Eisenhower's optimism. But his sense of mission and optimism were rooted quite differently from Eisenhower's. He believed not at all in Soviet sincerity; his religion was no bland belief in people-to-people togetherness, but a stern distrust of the sinner, combined with the lawyer's zeal to outwit him and the determination of the *Realpolitiker* to overpower him. Dulles' pessimism turned to optimism not because he thought the character of Russian leaders had changed but because he sensed that their power had greatly deteriorated.[15]

Dulles began negotiations with Khrushchev even before he arrived at the conference. He publicly proclaimed that the United States was negotiating from strength and "that the agenda ought to include not only German unification but two items that would affect the very stability of the Soviet Bloc and system—the question of the European satellites and the question of the activities of international Communism."[16] Khrushchev strenuously objected to this maneuvering and Eisenhower "denied that he knew anyone who had said the Soviets were going to the conference in a position of weakness."[17] But in his

[15] *Ibid.,* pp. 166–167.
[16] *Ibid.,* p. 168.
[17] *Ibid.,* pp. 169–170.

testimony before the House Appropriations Committee on June 10 (not released until July), Dulles confirmed that he was approaching the Geneva Conference with an eye to exploiting the weaknesses of the Soviet system.

Davis concludes that the United States went to the conference with divided perspectives.

> If we reflect upon the respective aims and methods of the protagonists we see that three approached the conference wtih psychological means or purposes in mind: Eisenhower sought a new spirit, hoping thus to dispel the fear of nuclear onslaught; Dulles, in the Foreign Ministers' Conference, used psychological pressures to bring about substantitive changes in the power balance; the Russians sought a relaxation of tensions in the West. But all dressed them in substantive problems—the German problem, European security, or disarmament. Of these Germany received priority. The conferees were not sure whether Germany might or might not prove a pay-off, but they labored as though it might, since if the pay-off was to be substantive it could only be in this area.[18]

Because of his obsessive anti-Communism and his fixed notion that the Soviets were coming to the conference out of weakness, Dulles felt no compulsion to support Eisenhower's crusade for peace.

If the Soviets were as weak as Dulles seemed to infer, then there was some possibility that a firm but conciliatory line might have had an appeal to the Soviets and might have encouraged Soviet interest in a détente. Quite possibly, the United States had a greater interest in a détente than Dulles allowed. Changes in the world situation were calling for adjustments in American foreign policy and strategy. Europe no longer felt the compelling insecurity that had made its dependence upon the United States so absolute. The crisis in European overseas possessions that the Kremlin was moving so deftly to exploit called for greater flexibility and attention on the part of the United States. With the Soviet H-Bomb the United States was no longer immune to the dangers of a thermonuclear holocaust. These considerations might well have been explored behind a carefully orchestrated and controlled diplomacy of summitry exploiting the undeniable psychological appeal of Eisenhower's "peace offensive."[19] There was some positive advantage to using the Soviet desire for a

[18] *Ibid.*, p. 171.

[19] An excessive fear of a letdown in Western resolve and willingness to sacrifice permeated all discussions and reinforced America's unyielding diplomatic stance. It is hard to believe that the letdown would have been so immediate and sweeping as to make the West vulnerable to any and all forms of Communist manipulation.

respite in Europe to make adjustments in America's own strategic posture. Unfortunately Dulles chose to interpret Soviet motives and strength entirely in the light of his obsessive anti-Communism and to cling obstinately to the illusion that the Soviets were coming to Geneva out of profound weakness.

Because the Geneva Conference was the first postwar meeting of Soviet and Western chiefs of state since Potsdam, it had a particular significance. The attention it invited and the aura of publicity in which it unfolded meant that it would bring to focus not only the diplomatic positions but also the foreign policies and strategies of the major powers. Inevitably each side would attempt to use the conference not only to seek immediate accommodations but also to strengthen worldwide support for its long-term interests. It is this combination that constitutes the character of what Paul C. Davis calls the "new diplomacy." Because Dulles and Eisenhower were divided in philosophy, each acting in the light of quite divergent strategic perspectives, American diplomacy was hardly in a position to wrest the maximum advantage from the new diplomacy. Dulles' misreading of the strategic situation (Soviet weakness, for example) deprived America of the full advantages that might have accrued from the conference.

Eisenhower, meanwhile,

> . . . relentlessly pursued his aim of convincing the Russians of his sincerity and thus creating a "new spirit." In his opening statement, after outlining the difficulties that lay before them, he called upon the participants to ". . . create a new spirit that will make possible future solutions of problems . . ." and ". . . try to take here and now at Geneva the first steps on a new road to a just and durable peace." He had some nasty things to say about international communism, but he said them in an un-nasty tone. He closed the first day, in his capacity as chairman, with an appeal for a continued spirit of friendship and sincerity as they got into the substantive questions.[20]

The new diplomacy came dramatically to the fore with Eisenhower's "Open Skies" proposal.

> At the fifth plenary session, July 21, Eisenhower interrupted the reading of a memorandum to inject the following extempore statement:
>
> "Gentlemen, since I have been working on this memorandum to present to this Conference, I have been searching my heart and mind for something that I could say here that could convince everyone of the great sincerity of the United States in approaching this problem of disarma-

[20] Davis, *op. cit.,* 173.

ment. . . . I propose, therefore, that we take a practical step, that we begin an arrangement, very quickly, as between ourselves immediately. These steps would include:
To give each other a complete blueprint of our military establishments, from beginning to end, from one end of our countries to the other; lay out the establishments and provide the blueprints to each other.
Next, to provide within our countries facilities for aerial photography to the other country—we to provide you the facilities within our country, ample facilities for aerial reconnaissance, where you can make all the pictures you choose and take them to your own country to study, you to provide exactly the same facilities for us and we to make these examinations, and by this step to convince the world that we are providing as between ourselves against the possibility of great surprise attack, thus lessening danger and relaxing tension."[21]

The Open Skies proposal was essentially the product of psychological warfare specialists, who proposed it and the President's Cold War adviser Nelson Rockefeller, who in turn persuaded Admiral Radford and Secretary of Defense Robert Anderson to give it their support. Eisenhower adopted the idea. Even though by inspiration it was an offensive Cold War maneuver and therefore inconsistent with the "spirit of Geneva" it "achieved by the manner of its announcement an aura of apparent spontaneity."[22] Even the Russians "went along with the myth of sincerity, apparently for two reasons: first, they wanted to salvage the 'spirit' and second they were caught on the horns of a dilemma and knew it. To have openly rejected the proposal immediately would have been foolhardy, for the world's press took the proposal to heart; it was a great psychological coup."[23]

Had the Open Skies proposal been pursued by the United States as an expression of America's strategy of reasonableness and as part of a disarmament and arms control strategy, it might have been more than a brilliant psychological stroke. Instead the open skies proposal was exploited exclusively for its Cold War value and then dropped.

Conversely, for all of the calculated opportunism behind Soviet exploitation of the "spirit of Geneva," the United States had just as much to gain as the Soviet Union. There was no intrinsic reason why the United States could not have pursued both a strategy of détente and a policy of firmness under the aegis of the "spirit of Geneva" much as Kennedy did a decade later. Being an open society the United States could give far more credibility to its professions of peace than the Soviet Union; open skies was a good indicator of the

[21] *Ibid.*, p. 174.
[22] *Ibid.*, p. 175.
[23] *Ibid.*, pp. 175–176.

relative advantage that the United States would enjoy in a peace race.[24]

Strategically and tactically it would have permitted the United States to adjust its diplomacy to meet the Soviet offensive among the nonaligned countries of Asia and Africa. The Soviets apparently looked for some unilateral concessions from the West to match those made by the Soviet Union to bring about the conference. At the subsequent Foreign Ministers Conference in October, Molotov "claimed for Russia certain unilateral deeds already taken in the 'spirit,' but made veiled assertions that others were seeking to obscure the success of the first conference and were failing to use unilateral 'opportunities' as benevolent as those Russia had acted upon."[25]

It is therefore difficult, Davis concludes,

> to explain how Eisenhower came to lose momentum in pushing an aim he could hardly have discarded so quickly. The seeming duplicity of the Russian mission to Cairo would appear insufficient cause to have abandoned his missionary purpose, given the fruits he hoped from it. It may simply be that as Eisenhower was not himself to participate in the second conference he lost interest.[26]

Thus the terrain so brilliantly won was turned over to the Communists. It was not a terrain congenial to either Dulles' temper or diplomatic forte. By contrast, "Russia had larger purposes for the 'spirit of Geneva' and kept it thriving much longer than did the West."[27]

The Soviets needed time and a favorable climate in which to launch their Afro-Asian offensive. Because of their military inferiority and internal succession problems, they were also interested in marking time. A properly conceived American strategy would have sought to exploit the psychological and political possibilities of the Soviet "defensive strategy" while adjusting its own strategy. The "spirit of Geneva" provided the psychological and political environment for such a maneuver. It was hardly to be expected that the Kremlin leaders would agree to aerial inspection of Russia or an end to the Cold War, but it did not rule out accommodations on other, less

[24] "Open Skies . . . illuminated the possibilities of symbolic negotiation. It revealed for just a moment the tremendous vulnerability of the Soviet Union to the well-conceived psychological operation: one which appeals superficially to dramatic and simple truth while it exposes beneath the surface basic flaws in Soviet society." *Ibid.*, p. 185.

[25] *Ibid.*, p. 181.

[26] *Ibid.*, p. 177.

[27] *Ibid.*, p. 178.

sensitive, issues. To execute this maneuver the United States would have to tacitly recognize Soviet control in Eastern Europe. Such a course was anathematic to Dulles.

> Secretary Dulles sought in vain through his (and Eisenhower's) negotiative propaganda not to reach accommodation, but rather to weaken the Soviet hold on the European satellites. He failed both because of Soviet negotiating tactics and because his objective conflicted with the President's. Geneva was a manifestation of the thaw in Eastern Europe, but the thaw owed far more to a Soviet decision to liberalize its controls than to the maneuvers of Dulles.[28]

Dissension Within the Soviet Bloc

On the surface it might appear that the Soviet bloc was immune to the divisive tendencies that constricted American diplomacy in the welter of competing economic, ideological, and political forces both at home and abroad. Was not Moscow skillfully dismantling the props of America's grand alliance? American leaders took small comfort from the fact that the Kremlin was acting more reasonably, when by so doing it extended Russian political influence by leaps and bounds. Was the Soviet Union really immune to the economic and political forces that made political leadership in the West such an arduous task? To those who believed that the new Soviet strategy was more dangerous than the old, the seeming ability of the Kremlin to switch to peaceful coexistence without mishap was discouraging in the extreme. The ideologues and journeymen practitioners of the Cold War arts were baffled by the sudden switch in their opponent's game. They had still to be tutored in the finer arts of political strategy, which were now coming into play. More sober analysts feared that the West was being lulled into a false sense of security that did not reflect any real change in Soviet goals and ambitions.

Robert Osgood sums up the spirit of pessimism with which those who respected the caliber of the Soviet performance viewed the new line.

> Measured by any realistic appraisal of internal developments in the Soviet Union and their relationship to foreign policy or of the altered international military and political environment and its relationship to Soviet *realpolitik,* these popular assumptions were extravagantly optimistic. In the retrospective view of the 1960's it was clearer than in 1955 and 1956 that the Soviet "new look" in foreign policy represented an imaginative

[28] *Ibid.,* p. 184.

effort not to stabilize the status quo, even in Europe, but to capitalize upon the growth of Soviet nuclear and industrial power, combined with the intensification of the nationalist, economic, and social revolution in the "underdeveloped" areas, to extend Soviet influence and control beyond the bounds consolidated under Stalin while hastening the disintegration of the Western alliance. Khrushchev might accept the existence of a military stalemate insofar as it ruled out the calculated resort to nuclear war or direct armed aggression, but he interpreted this situation of mutual deterrence not as a basis for political accommodation but rather as an opportunity to conduct political and psychological warfare more actively against the Western coalition and its vulnerable outposts like Berlin, while destroying the remnants of Western influence in the "zone of peace" and incorporating the uncommitted nations into a "socialist world system."

In this new phase of the cold war the deterrent to Soviet military adventures was probably as much Russia's opportunities for non-violent aggrandizement as her fear of nuclear retaliation. Yet Khrushchev's growing confidence in the shift of the military balance away from the West toward the Soviet Union and his willingness to play the game of nuclear blackmail and brinkmanship more adventurously in the Middle East and Berlin foreshadowed an increasing danger that Russia might also become engaged in limited military incursions, either deliberately or inadvertently. In any event, by 1954 the range of tactical options for advancing Soviet interests had certainly grown substantially since the death of Stalin, and this foreshadowed a period of intensified Soviet probing and maneuver. Therefore, the post-Stalin phase of the cold war clearly called for new strategic flexibility in order to preserve the military basis of allied security and cohesion.[29]

Unfortunately, the need for new strategic flexibility "to preserve the military basis of allied security and cohesion" went largely unheeded. In fact, the Soviet Union was not wholly immune to the divisive economic and political forces that play such a potent role in Western diplomacy. Western observers were aware that a succession crisis was occurring in the Kremlin and that all was not well within the Soviet bloc. Few people would have predicted in 1955 that in 1956 the Communist world would be shaken to its foundations by revolts in Poland and Hungary or that the men in the Kremlin would be driven to desecrate Stalin's image in order to free Soviet society from the legacy of terror that was stifling Russia's economic development. Khrushchev could hardly have foreseen the profound consequences that would stem from his decision to denounce Stalin in order to bring the leadership back into touch with the Soviet people.

[29] Reprinted from *NATO, The Entangling Alliance* by Robert Osgood, by permission of The University of Chicago Press, pp. 100–101. Copyright © 1962 by The University of Chicago.

Given the Communist emphasis upon doctrinal unity and tight monolithic control it would take years for the ramifications of Khrushchev's denunciation to become manifest. To understand what prompted Khrushchev's speech and what the consequences have been helps us to understand the immutable characteristics of the nation-state system and the limits that it imposes to the freedom even of a totalitarian system. For four decades the unity of the Communist world movement had been built around "the existence of a unique center of both political power and doctrinal authority—the Soviet Union."[30] This unity might have been preserved in spite of the rise of Communist China, had not Khrushchev felt compelled to make the "secret speech" denouncing Stalin. Richard Lowenthal explains why:

> . . . the chances of such success were critically impaired when Khrushchev, setting out to destroy the myth of Stalin's infallibility, destroyed forever the belief in the infallibility of the Soviet Communist Party and thus precluded himself from inheriting Stalin's worldwide prestige. The shock of de-Stalinization was the direct cause of the East European crisis of October 1956; and although the Chinese Communists then worked actively to help restore Soviet leadership, in the hope of decisively influencing its future use, they never forgot that it rested henceforth on borrowed authority. The "secret speech" was certainly not the original cause of the Sino-Soviet conflict, as the Chinese have since claimed; but by damaging beyond repair the traditional prestige of the Soviet Communist Party, it provided the basis for Peking's challenge to Moscow's worldwide leadership, which was to turn that conflict into a schism.
>
> The emergence of a plurality of sovereign Communist powers, and the vacuum of international authority created by de-Stalinization, were thus basic factors in making the disintegration of the organization and doctrine of world Communism possible: given these two conditions, any major differences of national interest and internal ideological needs between the two principal Communist powers might lead to open political and doctrinal conflict between them, for each would now decide its policies independently and seek to justify them in ideological terms. The only way to maintain a modicum of unity within this new pluralistic constellation would have been a common effort to tolerate the inevitable political and doctrinal differences, to develop a looser form of international cooperation based on pragmatic compromise and ideological nonaggression. This

[30] Lowenthal, Richard, "The Prospects for Pluralistic Communism" in Milorad Drachkovitch, ed., *Marxism in the Modern World* (Stanford: Stanford University Press, 1965), p. 226, with the permission of the publishers, Stanford University press, © 1965 by the Board of Trustees of the Leland Stanford Junior University. A documentary history of the Sino-Soviet dispute beginning with an extract from Khrushchev's Twentieth Congress Speech and continuing down to 1961 is to be found in *The Sino-Soviet Dispute,* G. F. Hudson (ed.) published by *The China Quarterly.*

would have required that neither Moscow nor Peking claim a position of world leadership founded on a monopoly of orthodoxy for its own interpretation of the doctrine; for such claims, being no longer based on unique power or unquestioned tradition, could now be made with equal justification by either side, and could only lead to mutual accusations of heresy. But once such accusations were publicly raised in the forum of the international Communist movement, not only the international influence of the Soviet and Chinese leaders but even the legitimacy of their rule in their own empires would be at stake in the factional struggle thus opened —and this would make retreat and compromise impossible and organizational and doctrinal schism inevitable.[31]

Only the most profound reasons would have prompted Khrushchev to embark upon so dangerous a road. The system of rule that had enabled Stalin to weld an empire and menace the West had only been at a price—"Soviet society could not develop further without a drastic change in the methods of governing it. . ."[32] Again Lowenthal offers a convincing description of the dynamics that forced Khrushchev's decision.

Under Stalin, the creation of the material skeleton of an industrial society had been accompanied by periodic violent transformations of the social structure, these "revolutions from above," intended in theory as thrusts toward the goal of a classless society, served in practice to prevent any consolidation of the body social that might weaken the power of the totalitarian state. Toward the end of his life, Stalin had proclaimed that the achievement of true communism would require, apart from quantitative advances in productivity and corresponding increases of real income and reductions of working time, one more major structural change: the transformation of collective farm property into all-national property, which would end the distinction between collective farms and state farms, between collective peasants and state workers.

As late as the Twenty-first Party Congress in 1959, Khrushchev, in outlining his own program for the building of communism, accepted the disappearance of the distinction between collective farms and state farms as a precondition for reaching the goal, and he announced a catalogue of measures aimed at bringing about this structural change. Yet while Stalin had envisaged an abolition of all monetary exchanges between the collective farms and the state and their replacement by barter contracts as the crucial step in this transformation, Khrushchev's reforms had tended for years to raise agricultural productivity by making all costs and prices comparable in monetary terms; and he showed himself anxious to accomplish the new structural change without a setback in productivity, hence without violent upheaval. In short, Khrushchev was seeking to combine the dynamics of ever-new structural change, required by Com-

[31] *Ibid.*, pp. 227–228.
[32] *Ibid.*, p. 230.

munist doctrine, with the dynamics of economic rationality, imposed by competition with the non-Communist world at the stage of development reached by Soviet society; and experience soon showed that the two were in conflict, for every local advance in structural change promptly resulted in losses in agricultural output.[33]

The West could not know this but the consequences were not long in coming. The relaxing of Stalinist tensions in Eastern Europe came at a moment when popular forces in Poland and Hungary were demanding a greater voice in the regime. The Polish situation at first was regarded as the more serious. The Central Committee of the Polish Communist Party (Polish Workers' Party) rejected the Soviet allegation that the mass demonstrations by workers in Poznan were provoked by hostile agents and wisely decided that the situation called for a change of Party leadership. Wladyslaw Gomulka and others who had been purged from the Party by Stalinists were readmitted, the workers' grievances were treated as legitimate expressions of discontent by the Polish Party press, and it was recognized that only a man with great authority and popularity could hope to master the situation without bloodshed. Consequently, the Central Committee backed Gomulka in a decisive showdown with Khrushchev and other Soviet leaders who flew in from Moscow. In the face of clear evidence that the new Polish leadership had popular backing and that the Polish Army would resist any attempt by the Soviet Army to suppress the new regime, Khrushchev backed down.

In Hungary, the popular outburst against the regime's dismal record was slower in coming. The new leadership of the Hungarian Communist Party under Gerö, unlike Gomulka, proved unable to master the demonstrations and violence. The leadership of the revolutionary movement passed to Imre Nagy who, instead of playing the role of the Hungarian Gomulka, acceded to the popular pressures, which were more anti-Communist than Communist. "In contrast to the Soviet-Polish Crisis, in which there was no immediate danger that the country might cease to be Communist controlled, the uprising in Hungary amounted, in Soviet eyes, to a cession of territory and population to the Western 'camp.' This the Russians understood to be so grave a danger to the Communist cause that armed intervention became inescapable."[34]

It seems clear that the Soviets were determined from the beginning

[33] *Ibid.*, pp. 230–231.

[34] MacIntosh, J. M., *Strategy and Tactics of Soviet Foreign Policy* (London: Oxford University Press, 1962), p. 176.

to undertake the military precautionary occupation of Hungary but that the decision to overthrow the government of Premier Nagy by force came only after Nagy declared Hungary's full neutrality and withdrawal from the Moscow Pact and after the American decision to take a firm stand against the British and French invasion of Egypt.

The ruthlessness of Soviet action appeared in the worst Stalinist style; the emotional reactions felt in the West together with the menacing posture assumed by Moscow in the Egyptian crisis, which occurred simultaneously with the Hungarian uprising, seemed to throw the world back into the darkest stages of the Cold War. We now know that the Hungarian repression was born of desperation and that the evolution of the Eastern European nations towards a degree of independence was merely arrested, not ended. Moscow was discovering that a world as complex as the Communist bloc could not be run according to the ruthless will of one man at the center. Its overall management and efficiency required some devolution of authority to the proconsular regimes in Warsaw, Prague, and Budapest. But Moscow could not afford to have the overall security of its empire threatened. Once the satellites understood the limits of their freedom the process would be permitted to go forward. But the outcome of any process as monumental as devolution within an empire is not in the final analysis predictable. A course, now called polycentrism, had been set; no man could predict its final destination.

Dissension Within the Western Bloc

Just when the Communist bloc was being shaken by massive internal contradictions, the West too was shaken by its most traumatic postwar crisis. The Suez crisis fused conflicting trends and forces within the Western alliance into a political nightmare. In June 1956, under the Anglo-Egyptian Agreement, Britain withdrew its troops from the Suez Canal Zone. A month later the United States withdrew its offer of a 56 million dollar loan to build a new dam on the Nile at Aswan and on July 26 Nasser issued a decree vesting ownership of the Suez Canal in the Egyptian government.

One setback after another in their efforts to salvage something of their former empires had strained the nerves of the British and French to the breaking point. The French government has just been defeated in Indochina and was now beset by a hopeless struggle in Algeria; the British impotence had been revealed by Nasser's bold seizure of the Suez Canal. The circumstances under which both governments labored were not conducive to rational examination of the alternatives. Strategic and emotional considerations combined to dictate one response to their plight: force. Eden, ill with strain, was goaded by an emotional obsession with Nasser. Mollet, the French Premier, had a more clear-headed strategic objective in mind—to destroy Nasser and thereby cut off the flow of Communist-bloc arms to the Algerian rebels.

Dulles, preoccupied with Cold War strategy, neglected and discounted Anglo-French obsessions. Dulles had agreed with Eden that Nasser must be forced to "disgorge" his illicit gain, but Dulles had no intention of countenancing force. At a moment of extreme depression in the national life of America's two foremost allies, Dulles showed himself insensitive and, in Eden's mind, arrogant and deceitful. As a result the French and British drew apart from the United States and took counsel only with themselves. Israel, fearing the buildup of Soviet arms in the hands of Egypt and smarting under Egyptian border raids, launched a campaign against the Egyptians in the Sinai. It met with great success. On October 31st the British and French, ostensibly to protect the Canal but in reality to overthrow Nasser, launched a military attack upon Egypt. The United States might have stood by and barred the road to Russian intervention. However, this would have lost United States support among the Afro-Asian nations and put it in the position of condoning aggression.

Instead the assault on Egypt, coming at the climax of the 1956 Presidential campaign, evoked the most profound antagonism in Washington. True, Britain and France had to be checked; or else the Soviet Union would have appeared the sole champion of Arab aspirations. United States support of nationalism and peaceful change had to be vindicated even against one's allies. Dulles' style was moralistic and heavy-handed. A biographer sympathetic to Dulles describes his reaction to the Anglo-French attack as follows:

> Once he had decided to oppose (the Anglo-French invasion), he had to oppose remorselessly and ruthlessly. In analysing his motives for taking the lead against the British and French in the United Nations, therefore, many different elements must be taken into account. There was his own Puritanism, stirred by a sense of moral outrage. There was his impulse not only to defeat an opponent but to crush him. There was an irresistible temptation to use his priceless opportunity to prove to the British that they were no longer a great power which could act without America. There was his contempt for Eden and a desire to teach Eden a lesson. In addition, Dulles had his own views on actual policy to support. He had been against the use of force from the beginning and he must now justify his attitude. . . .

Lastly, on the one hand, he believed that the British were simply mistaken in their reading of the Middle East situation and they must be shown how wrong they were, while, on the other, he felt as so many people did, that, even in the detailed operational handling of the Suez invasion, Eden and Mollet had behaved with a sickening disregard for morality and truth.[35]

The impact of the Suez crisis upon Soviet-American relations was profound. Moscow was able to pose as the champion of Arab aspirations against the imperialist West and to launch its peaceful coexistence offensive into the Middle East under unprecedentedly favorable circumstances. The Atlantic Alliance was shaken to its foundations. The British, and especially the French, were never to forgive Washington for their Suez experience. The Western alliance would recover temporarily—American support was still too valuable to France in its Algerian ordeal to be given up lightly. But their experience reinforced French interest in European Union and the idea of a European Economic Union (the Common Market). Suez should have been followed by an immense effort on Washington's part to reconstitute European-American relations to take account of Europe's renewed pride and strength. This effort would have required adjustments of thinking and innovations that the Administration in Washington was not equipped to produce. The temper and the routine into which the Administration had settled with its emphasis on military power and brinkmanship were not hospitable to political thinking and innovation.

Europe: North Atlantic Treaty Relations

In NATO, Dulles inherited America's highly successful experiment in alliance diplomacy. In truth it had become more than an experiment; it had become the center of free world strength and cooperation, a headstone marking the burial ground of the Marxist-Leninist notion that the advanced capitalist countries are fated to internal contradictions that drive them into competition and war. In order to tie Germany more securely to the West and to secure a German contribution to NATO, France had proposed to form a common European defense force in which French and German national units would be under a supranational command. But upon closer examination the European Defense Community had aroused intense political

[35] Goold-Adams, *op. cit.*, p. 239.

opposition in France: Why should France give up its sovereignty while Britain and the United States remained free?

Presumably Dulles and the new Administration should have been prepared to re-examine a policy that was not acceptable and either come up with new proposals or drop the matter entirely. But this is just what Dulles did *not* do. EDC was in all probability doomed before Dulles assumed office; it was foolish of him to resort to threats. Thus he told a meeting of the North Atlantic Council on December 14, 1953, "If . . . the European Defense Community should not become effective; if France and Germany remain apart so that they would again be potential enemies, then indeed there would be grave doubt whether continental Europe could be made a place of safety. That would compel an *agonizing reappraisal* of basic United States policy."[36]

The French National Assembly responded to this attitude by rejecting the EDC treaty by a vote of 319 to 264. The situation was retrieved by the brilliant initiative of British Foreign Minister, Sir Anthony Eden. At a nine-power conference in London, Eden secured approval for a new scheme for West German military participation in NATO within a restored Western European Union. This plan provided for the creation of a German national military force under safeguards that would prevent her from pursuing an independent military policy. The French Premier, Pierre Mendes-France, endorsed WEU before the French National Assembly and that body approved the agreements on December 28 by an exceedingly narrow margin of 287 to 260. Perhaps the French National Assembly required the shock of almost disrupting NATO to agree to West German rearmament. On the other hand, this experience with EDC should have served as a warning to Washington that the storm signals of French nationalism were beginning to fly. Long before de Gaulle came to power, the French Government was pointing the French nuclear program in a direction that would provide France with an independent nuclear deterrent.[37]

What was needed in NATO was a new departure, a recognition that Europe's status was changing and that if America was to retain its influence, NATO must be developed within a new political framework reflective of these changes.

[36] *The New York Times,* December 15, 1953, p. 14, (emphasis added).

[37] Scheinman, L., "The French Nuclear Program," (mimeographed) National Security Studies Program, UCLA, February 19, 1964.

It had always been understood that the defense of Europe must ultimately depend upon America's nuclear retaliatory power. The NATO powers were induced to make their precedent-shattering commitments to that alliance only upon America's promise that the Strategic Air Command stood ready at all times to implement it. Few Europeans even among those who revealed an interest in limited war strategies in Europe had shown any great inclination to relinquish major reliance upon total intervention by the SAC in event of Soviet attack. Military and civilian alike have appeared to believe that there will be no important war in Europe at all, or that the Great Deterrent will work because it must. For this reason European governments had never been willing to accept the costs and sacrifices of developing a large ground army in Europe.

By contrast American strategists from the very beginning of NATO manifested an intense interest in the establishment of large conventional forces partly for their utility, partly to meet European demands that they be defended not liberated, and partly to cover American divisions caught in battle. Strong conventional forces, for instance, might have had some utility for intervening in revolt-torn East Germany or Hungary although the United States never seemed to consciously consider using a strengthened NATO for that explicit purpose.

Confronted by a growing Soviet nuclear capability the Administration had to reconsider the wisdom of its primary reliance upon SAC to deter and to defend against Soviet aggression in Europe. It was apparent in 1954 when massive retaliation was enunciated that America would soon be vulnerable to counter retaliation. But massive retaliation was not phased out until 1957. In an article published in the October 1957 *Foreign Affairs* Dulles noted that

> . . . the United States has not been content to rely upon a peace which could be preserved only by a capacity to destroy vast segments of the human race. Such a concept is acceptable only as a last alternative. In recent years there has been no other. But the resourcefulness of those who serve our nation in the field of science and weapon engineering now shows that it is possible to alter the character of nuclear weapons. It seems now that their use need not involve vast destruction and wide spread harm to humanity. Recent tests point to the possibility of possessing nuclear weapons the destructiveness and radiation effects of which can be confined substantially to predetermined targets.[38]

[38] Dulles, John Foster, "Challenge and Response in United States Policy," *Foreign Affairs,* XXXVI (October, 1957), p. 31.

With that, the notion of limited nuclear war was launched as the basis of NATO strategy. Dulles did not mention that it was known long before 1954 that it was possible to make nuclear weapons of small yield suitable to tactical use.

The explicit application of the concept of tactical nuclear weapons and limited war to NATO strategy was made public by General Lauris Norstad in a speech in November 1957. In this speech Norstad reiterated the two previously accepted functions of NATO ground forces—that of providing a trip wire to signal massive Soviet aggression, and that of resisting the advance of the Soviet Army while SAC was devastating the Soviet homeland. To these Norstad added a third function:

> If . . . we have means to meet less-than-ultimate threats with a decisive but less-than-ultimate response, the very possession of this ability would discourage the threat, and . . . provide us with essential political and military maneuverability.[39]

Given the enormous thermonuclear capability available to both sides after 1955, the preoccupation of United States civilians and military with ground operations in Europe appears unrealistic. Ground forces that might have played an important role in the early years of NATO when neither side had many nuclear weapons, could hardly affect the outcome of a war involving massive strategic-nuclear exchanges. If American strategists had hoped to reverse this trend by persuading their Russian counterparts to adopt limited nuclear war they were sorely deceived. The Soviets warned that they would not limit themselves to a response in kind if tactical nuclear weapons were employed but would respond with the full range of nuclear weapons. One can only surmise that the faith placed in tactical nuclear weapons reflected an unconscious assumption that the United States was still in a near-monopoly position. The Soviets quickly succeeded in equipping their forces with tactical nuclear weapons and there is no proof that such weapons are any less advantageous to the offense than to the defense.

Above all the introduction of tactical nuclear weapons into NATO did a positive disservice to American leadership of NATO. It is hardly conceivable that the destruction from a limited war fought with nuclear weapons in a densely populated area like Western Europe could be limited. Tactical nuclear weapons rekindled Euro-

[39] *The New York Times,* November 13, 1957.

pean fears of a war fought between two nuclear powers on their territory. Second, the fact that the United States seemed to revert to the idea of a limited European war in which SAC might not be brought into play conveyed a subtle notion that the United States' guarantee was becoming less reliable in the face of Russia's growing thermonuclear capability. The introduction of tactical nuclear weapons in which the warheads remained under United States control exacerbated an already divisive problem within NATO. For some time the issue of control over nuclear weapons had been agitating European governments. The French in particular resented the fact that even though France was a leading member of the alliance, she was in an inferior position to Britain and America for lack of a nuclear capability. The Atomic Energy Act of 1946 forbade the United States government either to reveal its nuclear technology or share control of its nuclear weapons with other governments. This meant that the French commander on the Central European Front, Marshall Juin, did not know the nature and number of nuclear weapons he might have at his command. When this Act was amended in 1951 it was so worded as to permit the President to share America's nuclear technology and weapons only with countries already possessing a nuclear capability. This excluded France. Ostensibly this restriction was designed to avoid nuclear proliferation. As it became apparent that the United States was not going to help France become a nuclear power, the logic of French nationalism dictated that France should attempt to duplicate the British feat by developing its own nuclear capability. Consequently in 1957 the French government launched a costly atomic energy program designed to make France a member of the nuclear club. No serious evaluation of this development in the light of American national interest was ventured until much too late to offset it.

In France, once the common threat for which NATO had been created appeared to recede, the nationalist compulsion to remain a great power surged to the fore. Without a major effort to redefine the decision-making arrangements in NATO to give France a share in control of nuclear strategy, the United States would have little hope of directing NATO indefinitely to the support of United States strategic and diplomatic interests.

Britain, unlike France, continued to benefit from its "special relationship" to the United States. Britain's initial nuclear capability gave it membership in the exclusive nuclear club with the United States and the Soviet Union. When Britain found it could not afford to proceed with its missile, Blue Streak, it prevailed upon the United States to equip it with Skybolt and Polaris missiles. This special relationship, which Britain exploited so successfully, enabled it to perpetuate its role as a great power but at the expense of destroying its eligibility for the European Common Market.

Soviet efforts to exploit these divisions in NATO were not lacking. The Soviet diplomatic offensive of 1957–58 combined warnings of dire nuclear consequences, should war break out, to those countries housing American air and missile bases, with offers of a neutralized Germany and atom-free zones in Central Europe and other parts of the Continent. A Polish plan for a nuclear-free zone in Central Europe, first presented to the United Nations on October 2, 1957, known as the Rapacki Plan after its sponsor, Polish Foreign Minister Rapacki, next became a focus of considerable interest. Aside from its unacceptability to the West German Government, the Rapacki Plan was viewed with grave misgivings in Washington because it seemed to give the Soviets an undue tactical advantage. Its effect would be to remove American forces to the extreme periphery of Western Europe. As part of the proposed nuclear-free zone, West Germany would be at the mercy of large, conventionally armed Soviet forces. Such a situation would undercut the whole strategic principle of NATO which is to keep the defensive line as far east as possible.

The decision of the NATO Council meeting in Bonn in May 1957 to equip NATO forces with nuclear weapons gave the outward appearance of unity. It also meant the extension of tactical nuclear weapons into America's European bridgehead. Nevertheless, at the December 1957 meeting of the NATO Council, the American request to place Intermediate Range Ballistic Missiles in several European countries was refused by many of the members, including France. "In December 1957, therefore, the Soviet Government had to take into account a NATO Alliance which was about to increase its military strength and efficiency inside the 'bridgehead' of Western Europe," but which showed definite signs of stress and strain.[40]

Nuclear Deterrence: The Balance of Terror

America's comfortable belief that it enjoyed a permanent and commanding lead in the realm of nuclear weapons was shattered in

[40] Osgood, *op. cit.*, p. 119.

August 1953 by the revelation that the Soviet Union had exploded a thermonuclear (hydrogen) bomb. Winston Churchill told the House of Commons that with the hydrogen bomb "the entire foundation of human affairs was revolutionized and mankind placed in a situation both measureless and ladened with doom."[41]

President Eisenhower took cognizance of the implications for the United States and the world of the H-Bomb. On August 12, 1953, Eisenhower stated in obvious reference to the Soviet hydrogen bomb explosion: "We therefore conclude that the Soviets now have the capability of attack on us, and such capability will increase with time."[42] On October 6, 1953, he informed the public that "our former unique physical security has almost totally disappeared before the long range bomber and the destructive power of a single bomb. In its wake we see only sudden and mass destruction, erasure of cities, the possible doom of every nation and society."[43] This knowledge did not deter John Foster Dulles from enunciating his now famous doctrine of massive retaliation.

As long as the United States possessed a monopoly of nuclear weapons and means of delivery its nuclear capability could be used in much the way that weapons had always been used to persuade another nation to cease and desist from aggression at the risk of being destroyed. But with the advent of a Soviet nuclear capability the policy of deterrence acquired an altogether new meaning. Now neither side can afford to use its enormous power without knowing that it, in turn, risks nuclear annihilation.

Today deterrence means establishing the credibility of one's intention to resort to nuclear war in defense of a particular interest so completely that there will never be any occasion to do so. Deterrent capability is designed never to be used.

> One use of it will be fatally too many. Deterrence now means something as a strategic policy only when we are fairly confident that the retaliatory instrument upon which it relies will not be called upon to function at all. Nevertheless that instrument has to be maintained at a high pitch of efficiency and readiness and constantly improved. . . . In short we expect the system to be always ready to spring while going permanently unused.[44]

[41] Statement to the House of Commons, December 1, 1954 (Parliamentary Debates [Commons], DXXXV, 176).

[42] *The New York Times,* August 13, 1953, p. 1.

[43] Department of State *Bulletin,* XXIX, (Oct. 19, 1953), pp. 507–508.

[44] Brodie, Bernard, *Strategy in the Missile Age* (Princeton: Princeton University Press, 1965), pp. 272–273.

The two greatest problems of a strategy of nuclear deterrence have been that of establishing its credibility and its stability. The credibility of an American decision to meet an attack upon the United States or Western Europe with a nuclear riposte was probably well established in Soviet minds by 1950 if not earlier. The main criticism of massive retaliation was that it undertook to extend the threat of nuclear retaliation to acts committed in peripheral areas where the enemy might doubt the firmness of the United States' intentions. American strategy teetered on the horns of this dilemma all through the fifties. The Strategic Air Command held that the United States should focus on deterring Soviet aggression by concentrating on a massive first-strike capability designed to destroy the maximum of Soviet strike capability. Supporters of the Strategic Air Command argued that the only capability America could afford was one that could destroy Soviet nuclear forces before they had a chance to destroy us. In a sense it represented an attempt to prolong the strategy of massive retaliation into the future by enlarging America's counterforce capability. Because first-strike doctrine like preventive war, preemptive attack, and massive retaliation reflect what Brodie calls the ritual of liquidation—"the idea that some convulsive and fearfully costly act will justify itself through the elimination of the evil enemy" and therefore to "secure that liquidation almost any price is worthwhile"[45] —it was not consonant with the fact that the United States is a status-quo power and it overrated America's ability to get in the first strike. Other observers contended that psychologically and politically the United States was not in a position to execute a first strike and that such a strategy afforded no promise of knocking out enough of the enemy's retaliatory capacity to confine our own damage to tolerable levels. Unless we could unilaterally develop a substantial defense against the opponent's undamaged capability, then we exposed ourselves to the likelihood of being annihilated. Secrecy seemed to give the Soviets a first-strike advantage anyway.

In the light of these conditions the critics of a first-strike missile strategy argued that the United States ought to concentrate on a second-strike capability, that is, upon an invulnerable nuclear force capable of surviving a Soviet first strike and retaliating against the centers of Soviet population and industry. By always being in a position of holding over the Soviet Union the threat of annihilation should it resort to a nuclear attack upon the United States or its NATO allies,

[45] *Ibid.*, p. 268.

the Soviet Union would be deterred from risking either of these actions. The Navy and the Army espoused the second-strike strategy on the grounds that as the numbers, accuracy, dispersion, mobility, concealment, and protection of Soviet ICBM's increased, it would "become prohibitively difficult for the United States to possess the intelligence data and the striking force to give her sufficient assurance of substantially blunting Russia's retaliatory salvos."[46]

A first-strike strategy was also to be condemned because if each side continued to rely upon first strike, each would be driven to maximize the size of its first-strike capability in an effort to be certain of knocking out the enemy's entire second-strike capability. This thinking intensified the arms race.

Finally, it was argued that an American first-strike capability lacked credibility for the same reason as massive retaliation: namely, that American and allied opinion was against American initiation of a nuclear war against which it had no complete protection.

The Eisenhower Administration never made a clear choice between these two strategies either in words or in the way in which it developed American defenses. The announced strategy of massive retaliation—of meeting conventional attacks with a nuclear response—gave the Soviet Union a heavy incentive to strike first out of fear of being struck first herself. "The appearance of a doctrine of pre-emptive attack in Soviet military writings in 1955 lent further credence to the possibility of a Soviet defensive strike."[47] The ambiguity of America's deterrent strategy (first or second strike?) and massive retaliation added greatly to the instability and risks inherent in nuclear deterrence.[48]

In effect the Eisenhower Administration remained committed to the thesis that Soviet localized aggression would have to be met with nuclear fire power; because admittedly no nuclear exchange could long remain limited, the Soviets would heed the implication sufficiently to avoid all overt military aggression.

The Soviet Sputnik of October 1957 deeply reinforced the flaw that most detached observers felt in the American threat to meet every aggression by nuclear retaliation. Did the United States really mean that if a Soviet satellite attacked Yugoslavia or the Soviet bloc engaged in probing actions along NATO's southern flank, or that if

[46] Osgood, *op. cit.*, p. 188.

[47] *Ibid.*, p. 188. The Soviet doctrine of pre-emptive attack is discussed in Raymond L. Garthoff, *Soviet Strategy in the Nuclear Age* (New York: Praeger, 1958) and in Herbert Dinerstein, *War and the Soviet Union* (New York: Praeger, 1959).

[48] Osgood, *op. cit.*, p. 197.

the Russians or East Germans attempted another blockade of Berlin that the United States would retaliate with nuclear weapons and risk in turn a Soviet nuclear riposte directed against continental United States? As long as the Soviet delivery capability had been limited to manned bombers this potentially suicidal course could still be envisaged, but hardly when the Soviets possessed ICBM's with nuclear warheads.

Commencing with the Soviet thermonuclear explosion of 1953 and the American H-Bomb test of March 1954 an increasing number of American scientists were becoming concerned about the genetic damage that would result from unchecked testing of thermonuclear devices. During the middle 1950's their concern was limited to public protests and to demonstrating to their fellow scientists the inhuman and suicidal course upon which both the United States and the Soviet Union seemed embarked.

Those within the Administration who opposed permitting the H-Bomb's existence to become a factor in American thinking and planning, other than as a weapon, generally argued that its existence would not change Soviet strategy and tactics.

But as a matter of fact, it did have a profound influence upon Russian thinking. At first slowly and then with a rush, the Soviet leadership, especially after Khrushchev had consolidated his power, conceded, contrary to Leninist doctrine, that war was no longer "fatally inevitable" and that a nuclear war would inflict grievous losses on the Communist camp, even though Communism would survive and capitalism perish. Although the Soviet achievement of Sputnik would be used for whatever political or strategic advantages it might yield, it would reinforce Soviet concern that the new weapons not produce an uncontrollable military response.

For example, the Party's theoretical monthly, *Kommunist,* in September 1960 declared that:

> The working class cannot conceive of the creation of a Communist civilization on the ruins of world centers of culture, on desolated land contaminated with nuclear fallout, which would be an inevitable consequence of such a war. For some peoples the question of socialism would in general cease to exist: they would physically vanish from the planet. It is thus clear that a presentday nuclear war in itself can in no way be a factor that would accelerate revolution and bring the victory of socialism closer. On the contrary, it would hurl mankind, the world revolutionary workers' movement, and the cause of the building of socialism and Communism back by many decades.[49]

[49] Quoted by Zbigniew Brzezinski, "A Book the Russians Would Like to Forget," *Reporter,* XXIII (Dec. 22, 1960), p. 30.

Contrary to the assumption that Communist strategy would remain monolithic and uncompromising, differences began to arise with Peking over the significance to be attached to the new weapons of missile and thermonuclear warfare. Long before the schism between Peking and Moscow had reached the stage of an open break, the consequences of their differing views on thermonuclear war were already exerting an influence upon their relations—an influence to which the American Administration was somewhat unresponsive in its preoccupation with the earlier bipolar model of the Cold War.

Admittedly it took several years for the leaders in the Kremlin to publicly revise Leninist doctrine to take into account the military technology of the mid-twentieth century. And we now know that the tough and uncompromising obduracy with which Mao insisted upon Moscow at least threatening to use the weapons may have had something to do with promoting the Kremlin's decision to make the non-utilitarian character of nuclear warfare an article of doctrinal faith. Certainly Mao's reputed remark that good Communists would not flinch if faced with nuclear war because even if 300,000,000 Chinese died in it, there would still be 300,000,000 left to build Communism, must have given Khrushchev food for thought. Consequently, the temporary rapprochement between Soviet and Chinese Communist views achieved at the celebrated Moscow Conference of Communist Parties in 1957 was of short duration.[50] The following year the Soviet Union refused to support Mao in the matter of offshore islands, Quemoy and Matsu; or to use their missile supremacy in the Iraqi-Lebanon crisis or the Turkish-Syrian crisis.[51] Instead the Soviets revealed extreme prudence; Khrushchev preferred to exploit his triumphs in nuclear and missile technology in 1957 not as the Chinese urged to blackmail the West, but to cajole it into negotiations.[52]

On March 31, 1958, the Soviet Union announced that it would discontinue its nuclear tests provided all other nations ceased testing also. Although the main intent of Khrushchev's move was to influence the German situation, its implications were adverse to Communist China. In June 1959 Khrushchev cancelled Russia's modest aid to

[50] Even though a "peaceful transition" to Communism was still regarded as possible, a major addition was made to the list of forces whose growing power would prevent war—the national liberation movement. Hudson, *op. cit.*, p. 41–42.

[51] Khrushchev was called to task by Mao for considering Summit and Security Council Meetings in regard to these conflicts at which Peiping would not be represented.

[52] Hudson, *op. cit.*, p. 7.

the Chinese nuclear program ostensibly in order to improve the prospects for better relations with the United States.

Having just completed its own test series, the Soviet announcement was propitiously timed to put the United States on the spot. Either it would have to respond to the Soviet initiative or appear to be opposed to a moratorium on testing. In response to the Soviet initiative Eisenhower overrode his previous position against a nuclear test ban as an isolated step and his conviction that the United States should not suspend testing until it had learned all it desired to learn about nuclear weapons. Without prejudice to its right to undertake America's contemplated test series, scheduled for August 1958, Eisenhower announced that the United States would accept a two year suspension of nuclear tests provided that the Russians agreed to an international control system to cut off all future production of nuclear material for weapons purposes. Next the United States accepted the Russian proposition that a test ban should be negotiated and called for a new Geneva conference to negotiate a permanent nuclear test ban treaty. A number of changes of personnel and influence within the Administration swung the weight of the advice Eisenhower was receiving to the pro-ban, finite containment, arms control position; but in the long run the significance of Eisenhower's decision lay in the recognition that the need for some form of arms control to stabilize the military environment was becoming desperate.

The Geneva negotiations went on for eighteen months, first among the scientists and then among the diplomats. Certain technical criteria concerning the threshold at which on-site inspection would be appropriate were agreed upon but the Soviets chose to regard the American figure of 120 inspections as too high and the United States chose to regard the Soviet figure of three as "grossly inadequate." Unfortunately, the 1958–1959 Geneva Conference failed to achieve its objective because the United States' price for a nuclear test ban was a measure of inspection that Soviet negotiators were unwilling to accept. The Geneva Conference was hopelessly deadlocked by June 1960 so it is *not* accurate to say that it was a victim of the collapse of the Paris Summit meeting. Nevertheless it adjourned permanently that summer and the Soviet Union callously reverted to all-out testing in the autumn of the same year. Though it failed in its major purpose, the seriousness with which both sides approached the Geneva negotiations signified a genuine appreciation of the risks entailed in unlimited testing and nuclear instability.

Extension of the Cold War to the Underdeveloped Countries

The East-West struggle was not the only conflict unleashed by the political upheaval of World War II. Peace did not come everywhere with the defeat of the Axis; in many parts of the world hostilities became transformed into wars for national independence. The struggle between the revolutionary nationalism of Asia, Africa, and the Middle East and the waning empires of Europe has been an almost constant feature of the postwar era.

During the immediate postwar period the interconnection between the East-West struggle and the nationalism-colonialism conflicts was not fully realized. This lack of recognition did not last long. The most important political development of the 1950's was the discovery that the two struggles are very closely and inseparably intertwined and that the interconnection between the two has increased as each of them has intensified. Because most if not all of these new states were in revolt against European imperialism and because they were politically and economically ill-equipped for statehood, they were prime targets of the Cold War.

The collapse of European imperialism was viewed as an inevitable stage on the road to world Communism. It was a harvest that Moscow had long looked forward to reaping. The "peaceful coexistence" strategy that the Soviet Union adopted in 1951 was specifically designed to exploit the possibilities of disrupting the hinterland positions of the capitalist powers in Africa, Asia, and Latin America.

At first, Soviet literature stressed the need for a class revolution and for embryonic proletarian forces to participate in the national revolutions. By the time of the 1956 Twentieth Party Congress, the peaceful coexistence strategy assumed a somewhat different form. "Three doctrinal adjustments were made by Soviet theorists. . . . First, the validity of a national revolution was acknowledged, that is to say a revolution which is largely the work of a national bourgeoisie and a national educated class. Secondly, it was now generally admitted that the achievement of political independence and status was itself an all-important milestone in a country's progress on the road to the Socialist revolution, and it came gradually to be suggested that a fairly long pause before the next step might legitimately be made there. Thirdly, it has become legitimate to think that armed conflict might not be essential to a national liberation movement."[53]

[53] Holdsworth, Mary, "Africa," in *The Cold War* (New York: Praeger, 1965), p. 195.

In practice the Soviet Union attempted to create a favorable climate of opinion in the underdeveloped nations and limited its strategy to that of establishing a relationship of dependence between itself and certain countries deemed strategically important to Russia.

The American approach to the emerging nations was a facile derivative of national experience and unexamined assumptions. Americans took it for granted that because the United States supported movements for national self-determination among the Afro-Asian people that they would be responsive to American leadership. There was a rather naive tendency to believe that freedom would provide all that was needed to promote successful national existence and serve as an antidote to Communism.

To help the fledgling states through the post-emancipation period and at the same time assure America of their support, Washington devised a strategy consisting of economic aid and military alliances. It was not a well thought out strategy. It failed to take account of the intense distrust and hostility that the newly emancipated states would feel toward any ties with the West and the degree to which the United States would be identified with "white imperialism."

Americans tend to be unaware of the degree to which their economic and military aid has been tied to the acquisition of military rights and bases or to outright alliance. The Soviet Union has attempted to create a climate of opinion in the underdeveloped world; the United States and its European allies to preserve or reinstitute a position of power. As a result, the United States has failed to match the Soviet adaptability to the political realities of the so-called "third world." The Soviets have succeeded in accommodating to the conservative nationalist and social forces as well as the revolutionary; the United States has not succeeded in adopting a strategy of comparable scope or effectiveness.

Instead Dulles condemned India and other nations preferring to pursue a policy of non-alignment as immoral. He gave voice to this philosophy in a speech at Iowa State College in 1956. Dulles observed that America's bilateral treaties with forty-two countries "abolish, as between the parties, the principle of neutrality, which pretends that a nation can best gain safety for itself by being indifferent to the fate of others. This has increasingly become an obsolete conception, and, except under very exceptional circumstances, it is an immoral and shortsighted conception."[54] This attitude clearly limited America's ability to influence the nonaligned nations.

[54] Department of State *Bulletin,* Vol. 34 (1956), p. 999.

Foreign Aid

Foreign aid constituted an important adjunct of American Cold War policy. Although the avowed purpose of the United States aid program has been to help the emerging countries develop their economies, the bulk of United States assistance during the 1950's went to countries and for purposes directly related to American security interests. The allegation that the United States gives more aid to neutralist nations than to its allies is simply not true. Economic and military aid went principally to those countries that aligned themselves most closely with the United States in the struggle against the Communist bloc.

Non-European Countries Receiving American Foreign Aid[55]

Country	Aid in Millions
South Korea	$3,056
Japan	2,557
India	2,158
South Vietnam	1,440
Taiwan	1,865
Pakistan	1,160
Philippines	998

Of the countries that had received a billion or more in American foreign aid as of December 31, 1961, with the exception of India all were the United States' best allies in the developing world.

Beginning in the mid-fifties the Soviet Bloc began to match or emulate the United States with an aid program of its own. Examination of the Soviet bloc aid program shows that it differed somewhat in focus and motive from the American. Communist aid has been concentrated on a relatively few countries. Joseph Berliner provides the following estimates of total non-military aid from the Communist Bloc between 1953 and 1957.

The magnitude of the aid given to the first five countries as compared with remainder indicates a much heavier Soviet interest in the first group.

One authority suggests that the concentration of Soviet non-military aid indicates that the Soviet motivation is essentially strategic and

[55] U.S. Commerce Department, *Statistical Abstract of the United States* (Washington, D. C., 1962), Material from Table 1204, pp. 865–867.

Non-Military Aid from Communist Bloc, 1953–1957[56]

Country	Aid in Millions	Per Cent
India	$362	32%
Egypt	213	19
Syria	184	17
Afghanistan	115	10
Indonesia	113	10
Ceylon	26	12
Cambodia	22	12
Burma	22	12
Turkey	21	12
Argentina	15	12
Paraguay	13	12
Nepal	5?	12
Lebanon	2?	12
Yemen	2?	12

that it aims at creating a relationship of dependency between the Soviet Union and those countries strategically vital to her.[57] Aside from India, which has been wooed by Russia as well as the United States, the lion's share of Communist bloc assistance has gone to Afghanistan with whom the Soviet Union shares a strategic frontier and through which the Soviet Union might someday penetrate into the Indian subcontinent, to Indonesia, and to select Middle Eastern states. The bulk of U. S. aid in the Middle East went to Turkey, Iran, and Pakistan; Soviet aid went to Syria and Egypt strategically located just to the south.

During the early 50's American aid was essentially viewed as an instrument for aligning nations against Communism. According to the logic of this a polarization of countries economically aligned with either the Communist or American bloc should have emerged. Instead neutralism was developed as a means of avoiding alignment and at the same time extracting economic and military aid from both nations. If the United States and/or the Soviet Union expected to create a relationship of dependency on the part of recipients both were doomed to disappointment. In principle both the United States and the Soviet Union recognize that they cannot hope to capture a monopoly of influence.

[56] Berliner, Joseph S., *Soviet Economic Aid* (New York: Praeger, 1958), Table I, pp. 33.

[57] Beim, David, "The Communist Bloc and the Foreign·Aid Game," *Western Political Quarterly*, December 1965, p. 791.

CHAPTER 3

The Breakdown of Bipolarity

While both the United States and the Soviet Union continued to strain against each other in the arms race, at Berlin, in the Middle East, and elsewhere, new problems began to confront the policymakers in both capitals. We have already noted the important symbolic and practical consequences of the Soviet rejection of the doctrines that a major war was inevitable and that the capitalist world would suffer more than the Communist in an atomic war. Within the Communist camp these pronouncements were the visible part of a reef upon which the Communist bloc was slowly sundering. The steady development of Soviet scientific, economic, and technical capabilities had brought Russia to the apogee of its postwar power. Sputnik symbolized the remarkable recovery that Soviet society had attained, despite the wartime devastation and loss of personnel. The Soviet accumulation of versatile military power constituted an important new factor in the range of Soviet foreign policy; Soviet views carried more weight beyond the immediate borders of the Communist zone now that they were backed by missiles and thermonuclear weapons capable of devastating the United States.

Nevertheless, the Soviet leadership was facing the same dilemma as the leadership in Washington. In the first place, the new military technology consumed vast resources that could otherwise be used to satisfy consumer needs at home and facilitate relations with the Eastern European satellites, which were crying for industrialization and greater scope for their economies.

Therefore, when Khrushchev spoke to the Twenty-first Congress of the Communist Party on January 27, 1959, he could rightfully claim that "The domestic and international situation of the Soviet Union has never been as stable as it is now. . . . There are no forces in the world that could re-establish capitalism in our country or crush the socialist camp. . . . The capitalist encirclement no longer exists for our country. There are two world social systems: capitalism, living out its day, and socialism filled with growing vital forces. . . ."[1]

[1] Translated in Supplement to the Summary of World Broadcasts (Part I) "Twenty-first Congress of the C.P.S.U.," No. 1: First Day's Proceedings, January 30, 1959, issued by the BBC, London.

The successful Soviet launching earlier in the same month of the cosmic rocket known as "Lunik" or "Mechta" and the announcement that the Soviet Union would begin serial production of intercontinental ballistic rockets gave powerful substance to Khrushchev's grandiose claims.

What the Soviet people obviously wanted to know was how their standard of living was going to be improved. Khrushchev did not dare to disappoint them. "The fundamental problem of the coming seven years," he told his audience, "is to make the utmost time gain in socialism's peaceful competition with capitalism."[2] All indices of production and consumption for the Russian people were to be stepped up; but where did this leave the Communist Chinese who were in the throes of a gigantic economic crisis?

Of what advantage was it to the Soviet Union to make sacrifices and take unnecessary international risks to extend Communism if, upon coming into power, the new Communist states refused to accept Soviet control and dictation? Sino-Soviet relations were fast approaching a point at which their divergent national interests would lead each to contend for the leadership of the Communist bloc. It would not be enough for each to go its own way.

"Let China sleep," said Napoleon. "When she wakes, the world will be sorry." Unified after a century of disunity and decay, China loomed as a colossus of Asia by the end of the 1950's. The enfeebled giant had found rulers worthy of her size and civilization. The Communist rulers of China brought to their task the zeal and skills that had been so long lacking. Once the master of their own house, the entirely natural reaction of the Chinese rulers was to examine the behavior of others in the light of China's needs and destiny. However much Russia had helped China get started, China's enormous needs and exalted ambitions soon precipitated a crisis between the two Communist states.

Beginning in 1958, Communist China reached a stage in its evolution at which its interests as defined by its leadership required that the Soviet Union support it in actions against the United States over Taiwan and accept Chinese codirection in the conduct of the struggle for world revolution. In effect, Peking expected to be supported by the Soviet Union and by the entire socialist camp in its efforts to use the favorable developments in the world wide balance of power to redress the unfavorable state of the Asian power balance.

[2] *Ibid.*

The launching of Sputnik and of a Soviet ICBM was poetically interpreted in Peking to mean that "the East wind prevailed over the West wind" and the time had come for the socialist camp to reassume the political offensive against the capitalist camp. The Chinese affected a supreme indifference, not shared by Moscow, to the consequences of overt and precipitate action.

Almost as if to punish the Chinese, the Soviets stepped up their economic aid to other Asian states and the Middle East during 1959, while ignoring China's desperate needs (made worse by the failure of the Great Leap Forward campaign). They lavished aid on India and carefully avoided taking China's side in the conflict with India over the disputed Himalayan frontier. Even more disturbing from the Chinese point of view was Moscow's eager pursuit of a Summit Conference on Berlin that clearly presaged the sacrifice of Peiping's aspirations in Asia. On April 22, 1960, the Sino-Soviet dispute was brought out into the open by publication of an article entitled "Long Live Leninism" in which the Chinese boldly stated their adherence to the doctrine of "the inevitability of war" and dismissed the argument that nuclear war was an unacceptable disaster for the human race. The article stated: "On the debris of a dead imperialism, the victorious people would create very swiftly a civilization thousands of times higher than the capitalist system and a truly beautiful future for themselves."[3] Though veiled in doctrinal dialogue these debates showed that an inevitable transformation had been wrought in the relations between the two leading Communist powers. The divisive force of national interest was reasserting itself.

Instead of there being only two power centers—Moscow and Washington—two others—Peiping and Paris—still embryonic in form, could be seen emerging in the late 1950's. As they tried to break out of their bloc and take form, they would divert an increasing amount of Soviet and American attention away from their conflict with each other.

The United States too was beginning to experience a serious loss in its capacity to control the international environment. Obviously, the Soviet achievement of Sputnik and virtual military parity with the United States measurably reduced America's unique postwar position. Besides, now that America no longer enjoyed a decisive superiority, an uncontrolled nuclear arms race became increasingly dangerous. As long as the Cold War continued, both sides would have to be wary of putting the other in an impossible position.

[3] "Long Live Leninism!" *Red Flag,* April 16, 1960. Translated in *Peking Review* No. 17, 1960.

The U.S. Gold Crisis

By the late 1950's, the United States was also suffering a loss of financial power relative to other members of the Atlantic bloc and therefore relative to its ability to use that bloc against the Communist bloc on American terms. Throughout the postwar era, America's position of political leadership of the Western world had been buttressed by its economic power; in fact, without the scores of billions in economic loans and assistance, the free world might never have recovered and certainly would not have achieved the degree of recovery that was evident in Western Europe and Japan. America's economic strength supplemented and reinforced its political leadership. As long as the European societies were dependent upon the United States economically, they could not afford to take a markedly independent political line.

For years America had been exporting more to the rest of the world than it imported; other countries had covered their deficit to the United States with the proceeds they derived from American grants and loans. America began experiencing a severe deficit in its balance of payments.

United States Balance of Payments: 1958–60[4]

Year	Balance of Payment Deficit	Gold Sales	Increase of Foreign-Owned Short-Term Assets	Increase in Foreign-Owned U.S. Government Securities
1958	3,477[a]	2,275	1,171	31
1959	3,726	631	2,426	669
1960	3,800	1,700	2,100	

[a] in millions of dollars

The causes of this balance of payments deficit are complicated, in part because of short-term or temporary stringencies facing the economy but apparently due also to long-term imbalances in the relationship of the American economy to the world market.

The deficit appears to be comprised of a fall in American exports to foreign countries relative to American imports (America may still export more but not as much more as it did in the palmy days when America was virtually the only market for many items); a greatly increased propensity on the part of American companies and in-

[4] Harris, S., *The Dollar in Crisis* (Boston: Houghton Mifflin, 1962), p. 76.

vestors to invest abroad, i.e., set up or buy European companies to take advantage of lower costs and greater profit margins; and finally, the continued heavy outlays by the United States government for economic and military aid.

The balance of payments crisis that burst upon the United States in 1958 could have been anticipated. For most of the period from 1951 to 1960, the United States government spent between $6 billion and $8.8 billion a year for military expenditures abroad, military grants, and economic aid. The sudden decline in American exports relative to imports and the marked increase in the level of long-term private investment from an average of about $1 billion a year in 1951–1952 to an average of about $2.3 billion a year in 1958–1960 at least partially accounts for the crisis.

The political consequences of the crisis soon manifested themselves. The United States could not hope to continue to provide the economic means to support its worldwide policies with a major drain upon its gold and dollar reserves. From being a creditor, the United States was in a sense reduced to the status of a debtor—not in absolute terms so much as in terms of what it had committed itself to accomplish by keeping sizeable military forces abroad and by massive loans and grants. Such a transformation was bound to have subtle and powerful repercussions upon America's political position in regard to its partners and its ability to sustain its worldwide foreign aid and development strategy. Unless the deficit in its balance of payments was reduced, it would be dangerous if not impossible for the United States to continue pumping aid overseas that contributed to that deficit.

Abroad the balance of payments deficit appeared to reinforce the divisive influences operating within the North Atlantic Community.

France in particular seized upon the balance of payments deficit as a means to damage the United States' leadership in Western Europe. This policy is not unrelated to de Gaulle's efforts to reassert France's position as a great power by building up the European Economic Community (Common Market) at the expense of the United States and Great Britain. It is obviously much easier to do that at the expense of an economically vulnerable America than it would be if the United States was not suffering a balance of payments deficit. By instigating "runs" on the U.S. gold supply, de Gaulle hopes to reduce the role of the American dollar as an international currency to the benefit of the franc.

The French attempt to organize the Common Market against the

United States and Britain is in turn tied up with de Gaulle's determination to see France achieve the military and political status of a great power. Thus the United States economic crisis of the late 1950's is both part of and symptomatic of the transformation of the international scene.

Essentially the United States and the Soviet Union were reaching the limits of the politically and economically possible in their ability to manage and control their respective blocs. The level of demands upon their resources both domestically and abroad appeared to be rising at an exponential rate with little if any political gains to show for their massive outlays for military defense and economic aid to other nations. Both the United States and the Soviet Union were finding themselves challenged within their respective blocs by a major partner; both were finding the Cold War dishearteningly costly; and both quailed before the prospect of indefinitely raising the level of the Cold War with little if any hope of achieving a decisive breakthrough.

The Second Berlin Crisis

Ever since the mid-1950's, Khrushchev had been arguing that the growth of the "socialist camp" and the emergence of a large number of countries more or less sympathetic to the Communist bloc had brought about a fundamental shift in the world balance of forces; according to him, the victory of socialism could now be achieved without a major war. If war was ruled out as a means of achieving victories, then how would they come about? Khrushchev obviously had in mind that by widening and deepening the spirit of accommodation that he sensed in Macmillan and Eisenhower and by strengthening the hand of those who believed that the Soviets wanted to be reasonable, then concessions might be forthcoming, say at Berlin, which would in effect constitute victories and lead to other victories. It goes without saying that there were men both in Moscow and Peiping who disagreed with Khrushchev; the Chinese Communists did not agree in the least with Khrushchev's suggestion that the "ruling class" in capitalist countries might allow itself to be dislodged without a fight. They openly attacked Khrushchev's assumptions.

The core of their argument was that the policy of American "imperialism" and of Eisenhower, its "chieftain," could not change in substance even if it was temporarily disguised by peace-loving phrases: hence nothing could be gained by seeking an understanding with the U. S. in an atmosphere of détente, only by isolating this "main enemy" and putting maximum pressure on him.[5]

The Chinese bitterly resented the unconcern with which the Soviets brushed aside Chinese protests and the Chinese in turn sharpened their attack upon Soviet assumptions, especially the assumption that there was no longer any serious danger of war while capitalism still existed.

It was doubly important therefore to Khrushchev that his tactics not fail. Not only had Russia not succeeded in dismantling NATO, but the nascent European Economic Community was a disturbing new development. Unless Khrushchev's diplomacy could abort this latest manifestation of Western unity and vitality, the future would be clouded even if the Kremlin succeeded in evicting the United States from the Continent. What advantage was to be gained by excluding one form of strength if another was to take its place? The diplomatic and peace offensive of 1959–1960 was designed to secure recognition of East Germany and a modification of the Berlin regime both as a means of ending an embarrassing situation for East Germany and as a means of alienating West Germany from the Western alliance.

Unable to weaken NATO unity, to thwart the emplacement of American rockets in Britain, Italy, and Turkey, or to attract any NATO government to disengagement, Khrushchev decided to play his most dangerous card: Berlin. At a Polish-Soviet rally in Moscow on November 19, 1958, Khrushchev declared that the time had come "for the signatories of the Potsdam agreement to renounce the remnants of the occupation regime in Berlin."[6] Khrushchev also announced that the Soviet government would relinquish its powers in Berlin to the East German government with whom the Western powers would then have to deal. On November 27, Tass announced that the Western powers were being given six months within which to come to agreement with the Soviet Union for a free demilitarized West Berlin within a sovereign East German state. After May 27, 1959, the Soviet Union would no longer be responsible for Allied rights in Berlin.[7]

The Soviet Note of November 27, 1958, was tantamount to an ultimatum and as such was treated very seriously by the Western powers, especially by the Eisenhower and Macmillan governments.

[5] Hudson, *op. cit.*, p. 11. See also A. M. Halpern, "Communist China and Peaceful Coexistence," *The China Quarterly*, No. 3, p. 16.

[6] *The New York Times*, November 20, 1958, p. 1.

[7] *Ibid.*, November 28, 1958, p. 1.

Eisenhower in particular, while emphasizing that any war in Europe would be a thermonuclear war, showed a dread of a showdown and, with Dulles soon to depart from the scene, Eisenhower's views took on greater weight in the Administration.

As a result, the Western powers adopted a conciliatory attitude toward the Soviet ultimatum and agreed to a foreign ministers' conference, which opened in Geneva on May 11, 1959. The Soviets secured the seating of both East and West German representatives as advisers, which had the advantage of giving the East German regime apparent equality in the eyes of outside observers. Beyond that, however, the fundamental gulf in Soviet and Western positions soon manifested itself. The Western powers proposed that the Berlin problem be dealt with as part of a comprehensive plan for the reunification of Germany through free, all-German elections. The Soviets rejected this out of hand and countered by proposing the conclusion of separate peace treaties with "two German states," negotiation for unification to be left to them, West Berlin to become a "free demilitarized city," Western occupation to come to an end, and withdrawal of NATO forces and military bases from all "foreign territory." Not surprisingly the foreign ministers conference soon reached deadlock where it would have remained had not President Eisenhower elevated the conflict to a higher plane by inviting Khrushchev to visit America in the autumn.

The Khrushchev visit was the soothing part of the Khrushchev strategy, although Khrushchev never lost his refreshing candor in telling the American people that sooner or later they or their grandchildren would live under a socialist system. The diplomatic climax to Khrushchev's visit came when he met Eisenhower at Camp David, the President's retreat in the Maryland mountains. There Eisenhower conceded that the Berlin regime was an unnatural situation. The two leaders agreed that a Summit Conference should be held the following year and that the negotiations over Berlin, while no longer subject to a time limit, should not be prolonged indefinitely.

It is important to note at this point that Khrushchev's strategy had carried him to a point at which he was now dependent upon Eisenhower. What had begun as a strategy had gradually become real, because unless Eisenhower agreed to concessions on Berlin, not only would his strategy have miscarried, but Khrushchev's personal status would be jeopardized.

It is not surprising, therefore, that the Soviet press waxed almost rapturously over Eisenhower, the man of peace. He had suddenly become the man of the hour for the Soviet regime because if Eisenhower failed to live up to his word, not only would Khrushchev's prestige suffer but the Soviet leadership would be back where it started, that is, confronted by a critical problem with no painless solution in sight. Khrushchev must have seen Eisenhower as the vessel of his hopes and treated him accordingly. Eisenhower was endowed with the mantle of a genuine man of peace with whom the Soviet Union could have happier relations.

For a time after Camp David, Khrushchev could take encouragement from the sober spirit with which Soviet warnings were treated in London and Washington and from the evident difficulty the Western states were having in harmonizing their views as to the most effective means of maintaining their interests via diplomacy. The British argued that the only reasonable solution was to negotiate on the basis of an "interim" plan whereby the Western powers would make certain limited concessions to the Soviets on the understanding that their occupation rights in Berlin would be respected for a period of years. Adenauer insisted on an attitude of maximum firmness conceding nothing to the Russians on Berlin. Adenauer, who was opposed to negotiating about Berlin at all except in the framework of free elections and plans for settling the German question as a whole, was vexed by the conciliatory spirit in which British and American statesmen reacted to Khrushchev's campaign. This marked the beginning of West German disenchantment with Western efforts at accommodation with Moscow. But Soviet hopefulness turned sour as the State Department managed to firm up the Western position and give more and more vent to a tough line. Secretary of State Christian Herter on April 4, 1960, reaffirmed the Western determination not only "to protect the freedom and security of the people of West Berlin," but also to defend their point of view in other East-West matters. Consequently as the date of the meeting approached, Soviet and Western statesmen settled down to verbal exchanges with Khrushchev reasserting Soviet intentions to conclude a separate peace treaty with East Germany and abrogate Western occupation rights in Berlin. The Soviet leader was clearly showing his disgruntlement with the disappointing turn that negotiations had taken.

Whether planned or not, events now took an explosive turn. For at least four years U-2 high-altitude reconnaissance planes had made overflights of Soviet territory. Given the Soviet mania for secrecy and sensitivity to loss of control implicit in their inability to intercept the flights, Soviet leaders bore the situation in bitter silence. But suddenly on May 1, just two weeks before the conference was to convene at Paris, the Soviets succeeded in downing a flight piloted by Francis Gary Powers.

The situation was ideal for whatever purpose the Soviet leadership cared to make of it. It had been apparent in Moscow for some time that no gains were to be expected by holding the Summit Conference. Furthermore, the United States had been caught in a terribly embarrassing situation that was made even worse by subsequent fumbling in Washington and was climaxed by Eisenhower's acceptance of full responsibility.

Khrushchev was determined to use the incident to torpedo the meeting with Eisenhower and to do the most damage possible to the American position. In the presence of the world press he announced that the conference would not proceed unless Eisenhower publicly apologized. Whether he went too far in demanding President Eisenhower's apology for the U-2 as a precondition for convening the meeting is a moot point. Americans resented the bitter and vituperative violence of his tirades; but for Khrushchev there was no better way to save face at home than by using the occasion for a violent tirade against his perfidious "friend," President Eisenhower. No one had to put pressure on Khrushchev to rupture the Summit meeting in the manner in which he did it; Khrushchev had every incentive to do it just that way.

Khrushchev returned to Moscow by way of East Germany. There he told the East German Communists that they would have to wait "a little longer" though not "endlessly" for a peace treaty. The world was reassured to hear Khrushchev say that "The existing situation will have to be preserved till the heads of government meeting, which, it is to be hoped, will take place in six or eight months."[8] While the Berlin crisis was put on the shelf for a time, Khrushchev unleashed a worldwide Cold War offensive designed to exploit the bitterness that was sure to be felt among the masses over the affront to peace represented by the U-2 flights.

The U-2 incident and the collapse of the Paris Summit meeting under circumstances embarrassing to the United States was only part of a trend occurring in America's world relations. The development of the European Common Market, although essentially economic, represented a potential counterpoise within the North Atlantic community to America's leadership. French President

[8] *The New York Times,* May 21, 1960.

Charles de Gaulle, rebuffed in his demand for a nuclear triumvirate within NATO consisting of the United States, Britain, and France, was becoming more openly independent in his assertion of French national interest at the expense of United States' leadership. The stability of America's allies in the Middle East and Asia was severely tested. Military coups in 1959 and 1960 in Turkey, Pakistan, Thailand, and South Korea gave witness to the inherent instability of regimes that the United States supported at a cost of hundreds of millions of dollars. The renegotiation of America's 1951 Security Treaty with Japan, which was intended to give the Japanese government a larger say on the deployment of American military and nuclear forces based in Japan, provoked violent demonstrations among left-wing and neutralist elements in Japan that eventually forced President Eisenhower to cancel a projected trip to that country. In addition to difficulties with its allies in Europe and Asia, the United States was increasingly under fire in Latin America. In most of Latin America the rising expectations of the masses were fusing with exploding urban populations to generate revolutionary conditions. Everywhere the United States was the target of attack either for its apparent collusion with the traditional economic and military oligarchies or simply as a scapegoat. America's greatest fault had been in too long neglecting the problems of Latin America that were evident as early as 1945. Whether greater interest instead of neglect would have made any difference is a debatable matter.

The greatest challenge to America came in Cuba where Fidel Castro came to power New Year's Day 1959. Castro and his closest followers were imbued by a powerful determination to bring about a genuine economic and social revolution in Cuba. In doing so Castro's regime meted out drumhead justice to thousands of Batista's aides (many of whom deserved little more) and expropriated the holdings of Cuban and foreign capitalists. At first the United States government endeavored to get along with Castro, but a combination of Castro's revolutionary actions and propaganda attacks against America led the United States to lose patience. The result was a series of U.S. economic sanctions against Castro that reinforced his dependence on the Communist bloc. Whatever the explanation, it was plain for all to see that Castro confronted America with a revolutionary and strategic challenge on its own doorstep. A powerful breach had been made in the United States' century old domination of the Western Hemisphere. In meeting the Communist challenge it had generally been able to enlist sizable world support. Except in the

Arab Middle East and among the non-aligned nations, there seemed to be no major contradiction between America's security interest and leadership and the aspirations of the various countries. Suddenly toward the end of the fifties America began to experience difficulty in reconciling its security interests with its urge to act morally. The powerful changes occurring in many parts of the world provoked concern in the United States because they seemed to be directed against the United States. The easy assumption that America had a morally satisfactory solution to every problem was undergoing challenge. A new crisis of confidence began to overtake Americans. Beginning with Sputnik and culminating with Castro, Americans felt uneasy about their ability to act both to preserve their security and their moral leadership. As a result the Democrats approached the 1960 campaign determined to exploit the prevailing lack of confidence much as the Republicans had exploited a similar situation in 1952.

The great issue of the 1960 campaign was the alleged decline in America's prestige and here the Democrats had a tangible issue in Sputnik. Because of their excessive trust in military power, especially scientific and military technology, Americans overreacted to a momentary loss of superiority in one weapons system. In its election campaign, the Administration tried to put Sputnik into the overall context of the Soviet-American strategic balance, but it failed to diminish the importance of the Soviet space achievements in the voters' minds. The Rockefeller Brothers Report on national security and the reported findings of the Gaither Committee in favor of a greatly expanded missile and defense effort, including an increased limited war capability and a civil defense program, together with the sensationalism of much newspaper reporting on the United States' military capability supplied the Democrats with effective campaign issues. This was unfortunate because it drew attention away from the problem of revolution in the underdeveloped countries which was primarily a political problem. The great issue facing the United States at the end of the fifties was how to maintain America's security against subversion and at the same time not appear to oppose the revolutionary aspirations of people for a better existence. John F. Kennedy, the Democrat's presidential candidate in 1960, recognized the importance of this issue. His proposed Alliance for Progress, a program to assist the economic and social development of South American countries, showed considerable inspiration. The Republican candidate, Richard Nixon—like Adlai Stevenson in 1952—was stuck with the previous Administration's record.

CHAPTER 4

The Kennedy Years

JOHN F. KENNEDY entered the Presidency seriously concerned about the risks of nuclear war and disturbed by America's loss of prestige and apparent inability to convey to the world an image of hope and purpose. The youngest man ever to be elected to the office, Kennedy was the first President to represent the generation of Americans whose entire adult life had been spent in the midst of World War II and the Cold War. Of Irish background, brought up in a predominantly upper-class Anglo-Saxon environment, the son of a fabulously successful financial tycoon, Kennedy had become imbued at an early age with a sense of the importance of public life. The zeal that had characterized his career as Senator from Massachusetts had put him at the center of Democratic Party politics and had also whetted his appetite for the highest reaches of public life. The single-mindedness with which he aspired to the Presidency also made him deeply conscious of the uncertainties lurking beneath the surface of all social and political life. In social background, temperament, and experience Kennedy was similar to F.D.R. Both were "outsiders" to their class, both had supreme confidence and charm, both were brimful of the *joie de vivre* of those born to wealth and assumed position in society, both were superb politicians concerned to mold human hopes and aspirations into historic monuments, and both were decision-makers and innovators who surrounded themselves with bright idea men and intellectuals.

The intent of Kennedy's "New Frontier" program was to shake American foreign policy out of its increasingly conservative and unimaginative mold by imbuing Americans at home with confidence in their revolutionary heritage. The Cold War with its supreme emphasis upon national security and survival had thrown Americans back upon traditional and nationalistic values and reinforced the hegemony of a coalition of ultraconservative corporate wealth and the military over American life. At the moment of his leaving office, Eisenhower warned Americans that: "In the Councils of Government we must guard against the acquisition of unwarranted influences, whether sought or unsought, by the military-industrial complex."[1] It was natural to a man who had the utmost respect for America's traditional values and business leaders, to interpret the incipient

[1] *The New York Times,* January 18, 1961, p. 1.

garrison-state nature of American society in terms of the new scientific and military elites. But in fact, the whole society was becoming increasingly fixed and stratified according to materialistic, egoistic, and status values that were among the worst manifestations of a capitalist society. America's idealism and generosity were increasingly atrophied as more and more Americans became the beneficiaries of the new plenty and lost their concern for those who still waited to be admitted to the "good life"—the minorities, the economically impoverished and disadvantaged, and the hundreds of millions beyond America's shores.

The Cold War could not be overcome in a day. To Russia, Kennedy held out the prospect of a relaxation of tension through renewed negotiations on arms control and through expressions of understanding for Soviet concern about German revanchism. To Latin America, Kennedy tendered the Alliance for Progress, by which he intended to maneuver around Castro and prevent the spread of Castroism by getting at the root of the evil—the economic and social stagnation of the southern continent. To America's allies in Europe, Kennedy prepared to offer the prospect of a closer partnership in NATO.

Unfortunately one of those mechanisms from a previous stage of the Cold War had been left ticking away when Eisenhower left office. Approval had been given before Kennedy was elected for the Central Intelligence Agency to train and equip secretly a battalion of Cuban exiles to invade their homeland and overturn Castro's regime. Kennedy had committed himself in his TV debate with Nixon to free Cuba from Castroism. He now agreed to go ahead with the operation without being adequately informed of the risks of failure should the United States not actively support the invasion with air and naval cover. The CIA, in an operation which bore all the hallmarks of the irresponsibility associated with bureaucratic secrecy, deliberately misled the Cubans into believing that after 24 hours they would be directly supported by American military power. The result was a tragic defeat for the Cubans at the Bay of Pigs and a tragic setback for Kennedy's grand strategy. "Inevitably, it furnished grist to the anti-Yankee imperialism propaganda mill; it tempered enthusiasm in the new Administration and reduced its confidence."[2] It was also a stunning demonstration of the limits on the freedom of action of a great power and ought to have served as a warning elsewhere.

Tempted by what he took to be evidences of softness and indecision

[2] Freymond, Jacques, *Western Europe Since the War* (New York: Praeger, 1963), p. 179.

in Kennedy's stance and goaded by the continuing highly unsatisfactory state of affairs at Berlin, Khrushchev determined upon one more gigantic turn of the screw at Berlin. At his very first meeting with Kennedy in Vienna on June 3, 1961, Khrushchev repeated his ultimatum that either the West must accept a new regime for Berlin or he would make a peace treaty with the East German government turning over to it authority for Western access to Berlin. By once again renewing the Berlin crisis, Khrushchev was seeking to force the West to recognize that the power relationship had been modified in Russia's favor and to exploit the divisive influences already present in the Western camp.

Not long after Kennedy took office it was discovered that the alleged missile gap, if it existed at all, was only a lag in certain categories that was rapidly overcome. But Khrushchev hoped to exploit the impression of weakness generated by sensational reports of a critical missile gap.

Some Comparative Estimates of Strategic Strength[3]
(Early 1962)

CATEGORY	WESTERN ALLIANCES	COMMUNIST BLOC
ICBMs (over 2,000 mile range)	63	50 (minimum)
MRBMs (700-2,000 miles range)	186	200
Long-range bombers (over 5,000 mile range)	600	190
Medium-range bombers (over 2,000 mile range) including major carrier-based aircraft)	2200	1100
Battleships and carriers	58	—
Nuclear submarines*	22	2
Conventional submarines	266	480
Cruisers	67	25

* Includes both missile and hunter submarines.

Within the Atlantic alliance a significant shift in the balance of power was taking place, which de Gaulle was determined to exploit. Fundamentally the shift stemmed from Europe's phenomenal economic recovery from the shambles of World War II to a remarkable level of economic growth and productivity and to a renewal of European pride and self-confidence. The European Economic Community

[3] Cited in Freymond, Jacques, *Western Europe Since the War* (New York: Praeger, 1963), p. 197. Taken from *The Communist Bloc and the Western Alliance, 1961–62* (London: Institute for Strategic Studies, 1962).

binding the six continental nations was proving a remarkable success. United States exports to Europe still exceeded imports, but the investment possibilities within the Common Market and Europe generally were luring additional billions in American capital which, when added to the expenses of maintaining American military forces in Europe and economic outlays elsewhere, produced an enormous net outflow of capital and gold.

De Gaulle, no advocate of supranational organizations, suddenly found himself the surprised possessor of an unprecedented instrument for the furtherance of his political designs and ambitions. Roughly equal status for Europe with the United States and Russia in world affairs has long been de Gaulle's most fervent ambition.

The United States might have responded to the French aspiration for partnership by admitting France to a NATO nuclear consortium and sharing with France its nuclear and missile technology. This move would have made of France a nuclear power but would have been little different from the sharing that was already in operation between the United States and Britain. Instead, the United States preferred to preserve the nuclear status quo even though it was evident that de Gaulle was determined that France should acquire a *force de frappe* or striking force and even though it would embitter relations between Washington and Paris. As a result, de Gaulle was clearly in no mood to collaborate with Washington.

Renewal of the Berlin Crisis

The divided response that Khrushchev's renewed ultimatum on Berlin evoked among the Western powers was highly indicative of their differing perspectives. The American President had the awesome responsibility for controlling and, if necessary, employing America's nuclear power in event of a showdown over Berlin. For that reason, Kennedy was anxious to temper Khrushchev's blast by offering to negotiate to remedy whatever could be remedied without weakening the Western position. De Gaulle did not share Kennedy's view that the risks of war were great over Berlin. Furthermore, the French leader was convinced that Khrushchev was bluffing and that to negotiate under duress would be taken as a sign of Western weakness more likely to provoke Soviet acts of war than would a position of holding firm. The British, as usual more sensitive to public opinion and more inclined to measures of procrastination and compromise, pushed for negotiations. Almost by default the United States found itself with no choice but to stand firm while offering to consider any reasonable proposals. There being no Russian proposals that would appear reasonable or acceptable to the West, Khrushchev brought the crisis to a head on August 13, 1961, by the spectacular decision to erect a wall between East and West Berlin that would seal off once and for all the flow of refugees from East Germany.

The West German government was bitterly disappointed by the seeming impotence and evident unwillingess of the Western powers to risk war to prevent the callous fate of their East German countrymen. Kennedy demonstratively strengthened United States forces in Berlin and under the cover of the crisis executed a remarkable increase and shift in America's conventional military forces, but that was not sufficient to compensate Adenauer for the obvious blow to his policy.

West Germany had no choice but to stay with the West, but the obvious inability of the West to interdict Soviet actions and Kennedy's efforts to win Adenauer around to a more accommodating attitude toward the East German regime ended the illusion that German politicians had so sedulously nurtured of an ultimate unification of Germany on Western terms. The crisis came just when Adenauer was losing his personal grip over German politics, which further embittered his attitude toward the Kennedy Administration.

After confrontation between Soviet and American tanks at Check Point Charlie, the tension rapidly subsided. Khrushchev now switched to less aggressive tactics, but Adenauer remained firm. Adenauer had become thoroughly embittered by what he took to be an American sell-out; but he turned to Paris, not to Moscow to take out his pique against Kennedy. He recalled his Ambassador from Moscow on suspicion of lending too sympathetic an ear to Khrushchev's blandishments for a German-Soviet rapproachement and he leaked the Anglo-American proposal for an international access authority to Berlin to the press, thereby killing it at birth.

Khrushchev's motives for reopening the Berlin crisis are not hard to understand. The unsettled status of Berlin and East Germany are the last unsatisfactory aspects of the Russian wartime accomplishments in Central Europe. West Berlin is both a challenge to the status quo in Eastern Europe and the principal instrument by which Russia hopes to split the Western Alliance. In addition, the tactical situation had become increasingly intolerable due to the flight of hundreds of thousands of East Germans through Berlin to the West. And the renewal of the crisis at Berlin may have appeared to afford Khrushchev his last best hope for reversing the trend toward the progressive consolidation of Western Europe. He certainly could take little satisfaction from seeing United States influence diminished, only to be replaced by an economically and politically unified and resurgent Europe.

The decision to renew the crisis over Berlin may have been related to two other factors: the challenges facing the Soviet economy and the striving for a degree of independence by the Satellites. Whatever psychological and military advantage still remained to Russia from its missile achievement was bound to disappear as America accelerated its efforts in this field. Then, too, Russia's ability to deal with the growing independence of its East European satellites would be strengthened if it could secure unqualified recognition of East Germany and end the defections at Berlin. Finally, if Khrushchev could win diplomatic and other victories at the expense of the West, he would be in a stronger position to deal with Red China. Consequently, while the Soviet Union was approaching, if not already into, a period of adjustment to the new international environment that would lead to the partial test ban treaty and other manifestations of caution, it still had compelling reasons to wish to strengthen its position.

In spite of Khrushchev's best efforts at dividing and demoralizing the West Berliners and West Germans from their American and British allies, the outcome of the crisis resulted in a hardening of the Western attitude demonstrated by a refusal to tolerate sorties by Soviet armored cars into West Berlin under any pretext.

The Cuban Missile Crisis

Frustrated at Berlin, a situation had been ripening in Cuba that held out dazzling prospects. Ever since the Bay of Pigs fiasco, Russia had been pouring military equipment and personnel into Cuba. In an interview Castro told Claude Julien how Moscow had proposed to emplace missiles in Cuba:

> They explained to us that in accepting them we would be reinforcing the Socialist camp the world over, and because we had received important aid from the Socialist camp we estimated that we could not decline. This is why we accepted them. It was not in order to assure our own defense, but first of all to reinforce socialism on the international scale. Such is the truth even if other explanations are furnished elsewhere.[4]

[4] Julien, Claude, *Le Monde,* March 22, 1963.

It is now authoritatively accepted that Khrushchev's decision to risk moving missiles into Cuba was dictated by the opportunity to redress the reemerging nuclear and missile imbalance. Contrary to the image that had been created by Sputnik and by the alleged existence of a missile gap that had been skillfully exploited by Khrushchev (and by Kennedy in the 1960 campaign), "the bulk of the USSR's strategic nuclear capability has been effective only out to ranges of about 2,000–2,500 miles."[5]

Between 1961 and 1962, Secretary of Defense Robert McNamara had made it plain that whatever "missile gap" had existed was "a myth" and that the United States was possessed of an evergrowing strategic superiority. "Confidence in United States strategic superiority was restored in the West; moreover, it became apparent both from Soviet behavior and from the modification of Soviet strategic claims, that the Soviet leaders knew that the West had been undeceived about the strategic balance."[6]

The Soviet decision to emplace missiles in Cuba was made in the context of this situation. It represented a stopgap effort to recapture the substance of Russia's fleeting nuclear preponderance or parity.

It is also generally agreed that there was a connection between the exhaustion and failure of Soviet efforts to dislodge the United States from Berlin and the decision to emplace missiles in Cuba. In a footnote to his authoritative article cited above, Horelick observes:

> A link between the Cuban missile deployment and Khrushchev's Berlin strategy was suggested by the Soviet Government's statement of September 11, 1962, in which the USSR acknowledged that it was providing military assistance—though of a strictly defensive type—to Cuba, and warned that a U.S. attack on Cuba might unleash the beginning of a thermonuclear war, but at the same time declared a moratorium on new moves in Berlin until after the U.S. Congressional elections. (Pravda, September 11, 1962.) Khrushchev may have hoped to discourage any new U.S. action in regard to Cuba until after the elections (i.e., until after the MRBM's, at least, became operational), by offering, in return, to desist from fomenting a new crisis in Berlin, and then, after establishing a strategic base in Cuba, to use this new leverage to press for a favorable settlement in Berlin.[7]

[5] Horelick, Arnold L., "The Cuban Missile Crisis," *World Politics,* April, 1964, p. 374. There is a considerable documentary literature on the Cuban Missile Crisis. The most comprehensive is *The "Cuban Crisis" of 1962* edited by David L. Larson (Boston: Houghton Mifflin, 1963). *Collision Course* by Henry M. Pachter (New York: Praeger, 1963) provides a full analysis and documentation.

[6] *Ibid.,* pp. 374–375.

[7] *Ibid.,* p. 377.

The question then remains how Khrushchev thought that he could get away with the move undetected, and if detected, without evoking a challenge from the United States. In taking what appears to be a dangerously great risk involving, as later developed, the possibility of a nuclear showdown with the United States, the Kremlin was calculating that because of Washington's essentially prudent, cautious attitude that the United States would not launch a thermonuclear attack against the Soviet Union until all possible alternatives were exhausted. The United States acceptance of the Soviet Union's increasingly open military involvement in Cuban affairs after the Bay of Pigs "may have strengthened the belief of the Soviet leaders that the United States would engage in armed intervention only in response to the actual use of Cuba-based weapons against some Western hemisphere country."[8] Their confidence may have been offset somewhat by Kennedy's publicly stated warnings on September 4 and 11 that the presence of offensive weapons, even without any overt act, would be grounds for the United States to act. The United States, Kennedy warned on September 11, would not await some overt act but action would be forthcoming "if Cuba should possess a capacity to carry out offensive actions against the United States."[9]

The operation was already well underway, and the first Soviet ships transporting missiles are believed to have reached Cuban ports around October 8; the Soviets obviously still weighed the advantages over the risks favorably.

Having gone so far out on the limb, the speed, decisiveness, and magnitude of Washington's response was all the more of a shock to Moscow when it came. Time and again—in Korea, on the Yalu, in the Suez crisis, and at the Bay of Pigs—the miscalculation on both sides has come with startling force. Since such tests are substitutes for total conflict, it is not surprising that when they occur they generate enormous tensions. The Cuban missile crisis was no exception; the fact that nuclear destruction was for the first time a possibility for both sides imparted a life-and-death quality to the confrontation on a universal scale.

The character of the American response "apparently confounded the Soviet leaders."[10] By preserving a maximum degree of secrecy, the United States government presented the Soviet Union with a fait accompli; by imposing a quarantine, the United States shifted the

[8] *Ibid.*, p. 380.
[9] *The New York Times*, September 14, 1965.
[10] Horelick, *op. cit.*, p. 385.

responsibility for the next move to the Soviet Union and gave itself "more freedom of choice and action than the Soviet leaders probably foresaw."[11] The President's decision to ignore Castro and challenge the Soviet Union directly rather than involving the United States in a quagmire of reprisals against Cuba, as well as the speed with which he acted, threw the Kremlin completely off balance.

The fact that Soviet ships were approaching the quarantine zone gave Khrushchev no chance to play for time; the evident ability and determination of the United States to risk all-out war if necessary prompted Soviet fears that a United States attack was imminent. As a result, little time was lost between October 23, when Kennedy announced the instituting of the quarantine and the conditions for its removal, and Soviet efforts first (October 23 and 24) to reassure the United States that the Soviet Union had no intention of letting its missiles be employed by the Cubans and secondly (October 27 and 28) to announce its decision to withdraw the missiles entirely from Cuba. Khrushchev had his letter of October 28 to Kennedy broadcast over Radio Moscow to expedite matters because events in the Cuban crisis seemed to be outrunning diplomacy.

The confrontation was so total in its range and intensity—combining an attempted shift in the world balance of power with the threat of nuclear war and a testing of both systems—that it was bound to produce some fairly profound readjustments.

> By revealing the militaristic trends that continued to operate in Soviet policy, those events had raised fresh doubts in the non-Communist world about the feasibility of any lasting accommodation between Soviet and Western interests. "It is going to be some time before it is possible for us to come to any real understandings with Mr. Khrushchev," Kennedy had said, . . . "Mr. K. does not wish us well, unfortunately."[12]

Renewal of Soviet-American Arms Negotiations

The United States had been actively seeking some agreements on arms control that would serve both the immediate practical purpose of ending atmospheric testing and contribute to a political climate conducive to reducing the instabilities and tensions of the nuclear arms race. Khrushchev combined his agreement to liquidate the Soviet missile sites in Cuba with a call for renewed efforts to reduce the

[11] *Ibid.*

[12] Stebbins, Richard, *The United States in World Affairs: 1962* (New York: Vintage, 1963), p. 55.

dangers from nuclear competition and warfare. Kennedy seized upon Khrushchev's opening affirmatively. On December 19, Khrushchev sent Kennedy a letter containing some general disarmament proposals.

All previous efforts at disarmament and arms control had foundered on the efforts of the Soviet Union to use disarmament as a means of advancing its own special interests against those of the West. Nor had the United States been above attempting to secure agreement most favorable to its overall strategic requirements. But in the past, the serious pursuit of negotiations had tripped either over the Soviet obsession with secrecy or over the irresistible desire to exploit the arms issue for Soviet propaganda purposes. It had also been mortgaged on the American side by the obsessiveness with which the American military and elements of the scientific community preferred to keep the pressure on the Soviet Union rather than maneuvering for a shift in the terms of the Cold War away from strictly military competition.

Nevertheless, the disarmament question was again taken up in the wake of the Cuban crisis. Negotiations reopened at the meetings of the Eighteen-Nation Disarmament Committee, which had been set up in 1962. Still the Soviet delegate would not budge from the minimal position offered by Khrushchev in his letter of December 19, 1962, to Kennedy: a token number of two or three inspections a year on Soviet territory plus the installation of a number of seismic stations to record questionable activity for subsequent analysis. The main Soviet activity in the Eighteen-Nation Geneva meetings continued to be the propounding of proposals designed to embarrass and undercut the deployment of nuclear weapons under American or NATO auspices. Various Western plans including those involving the sharing of nuclear responsibilities with West Germany through a newly proposed Multilateral Nuclear Force (designated MLF) and the stationing of Polaris submarines in the Mediterranean were fiercely attacked both in and out of the Geneva disarmament conference. All the old threats of nuclear annihilation were hurled at countries collaborating with or participating in American nuclear sharing.

Kennedy pointedly reminded Khrushchev of what was at stake: "I am haunted by the feeling that [without a test ban] by 1970 . . . there may be 10 nuclear powers instead of four, and by 1975, 15 or 20. . . . I regard that as the greatest possible danger and hazard." On April 24, Kennedy and Macmillan joined in a special appeal to Khrushchev "to take a broader view and help get away from the 'numbers game' into which the test ban discussions had degenerated."[13] Unexpectedly, the Soviet delegate at Geneva belatedly agreed to Kennedy's "hotline" proposal for a direct link between the President and Khrushchev's office in the Kremlin.

Still determined to pursue the disarmament question and feeling that there was still some possibility for a new departure in relations with the Soviet Union, Kennedy "began to look for an opportunity to make a 'peace speech,'" which was given at American University in June 1963. Preparation of the speech was kept extremely confidential in the White House and shown only to the State and Defense Departments upon completion so as not to "set in motion a process of dilution."[14]

In this memorable speech Kennedy urged Americans to reexamine their ingrained attitudes toward the Cold War and the Soviet Union. "We must deal with the world as it is and not as it might have been had the history of the last 18 years been different."[15] In a brilliant application of the principle of "graduated unilateral action" to induce a comparable response from the opponent, Kennedy included in his speech the announcement that despite its past rejection of any unpoliced nuclear moratorium, the United States did not intend to conduct additional nuclear tests in the atmosphere unless others did so first.

Almost immediately Moscow gave favorable attention and Soviet jamming of Voice of America broadcasts ceased. Then on July 2, in a speech in East Berlin, Khrushchev took up a long-standing British-American offer to sign a treaty barring nuclear tests in the atmosphere, in outer space, and under water. The merit of this proposal was that such tests could be detected without inspection and any violation would become quickly known. The full extent of the Soviet conversion to an arms détente became known on July 19. Khrushchev gave up his conditions for a pact such as the withdrawal of United States forces from European bases and merely chose to view it as the starting point for a whole series of tension-reducing steps. "Among them he mentioned not only a non-aggression pact, but also the freezing or reduction of military budgets; measures to prevent surprise attack including the reciprocal stationing of military observers in East and West Germany; reduction of foreign troops in both parts of

[13] *Ibid.*, p. 70.

[14] Brandon, Henry, "Schlesinger at the White House," *Harper's*, July 1964, p. 59.

[15] *The New York Times*, June 11, 1963.

Germany; and, 'of course,' a final settlement of the German problem."[16] Even so modest a degree of agreement after so many years of Cold War seemed almost miraculous.

Significantly, the agreement was negotiated in Moscow almost within earshot of the ideological storm raging between Moscow and Communist China. The interrelation of the two events is beyond question. The treaty was easily negotiated and signed in Moscow on August 5, 1963, by Soviet, American, and British representatives. A hundred other governments altogether subscribed to it, although France and Red China were ominous by their absence. The test ban treaty by no means ended the weapons and nuclear competition between the Soviet Union and the United States. It probably represented a tacit agreement to shift the priority away from the development of weapons systems and the application of nuclear power to military purposes to science, particularly space exploration, and to civilian consumption. Vincent Rock, in *A Strategy of Interdependence,* argues that a complete break with the philosophy of the Cold War, which has overrated the advantage to the United States of all-out military competition with the Soviet Union, can only be achieved if the United States consciously seeks to shift the allocation of resources from a military priority to a consumption and science priority.[17]

Nevertheless, it is clear that insofar as the relationship of major tension is concerned—the twenty-year political and strategic duel between the United States and the Soviet Union—the United States has met the challenge. The Soviet Union now knows that it cannot hope to win in any kind of direct contest with the United States. Rather than risk nuclear war for marginal gains, it prefers to cultivate the possibilities of peaceful coexistence (Moscow, not Peking style). The management of polycentrism takes up much of Moscow's diplomatic and political energies. The Soviet Union has not abandoned its world design, but it must wonder if there is any point in taking considerable risks and sacrifices for a revolution that produces regimes who soon assert their independence of Moscow. The leaders in Moscow must be given increasing pause by the level of problems that they encounter within the Communist bloc and by the fact that Russia no longer enjoys exclusive direction and control over the movement.

[16] Stebbins, *op. cit.,* p. 75.

[17] Rock, Vincent, *A Strategy of Interdependence* (New York: Scribners, 1964).

Chinese Reaction to the Partial Test Ban Treaty

Peaceful coexistence and détente undercut the Chinese objective of isolating the United States as the one irreconcilable enemy. Peiping has done everything possible within the limits of its power to defeat the détente. In the midst of the Cuban missile crisis China assaulted an imprudent Indian advance into a disputed portion of frontier territory in a deliberate effort to humiliate India and force the Soviet Union to choose between a policy of support for Red China or support for a bourgeois nationalist government. Moscow, unable to support the extreme Chinese position without worsening its already tarnished reputation as a peace-loving nation, first condemned India and then fearing to lose its status as India's friend threw its support behind India and against China.

China's response to the Partial Test Ban Treaty of 1963 was even sharper. Being a nuclear "have-not" China had always been an ardent advocate of the "complete, thorough, total and resolute prohibition and destruction of nuclear weapons." The signing of a partial test ban treaty struck at China in a direct and potentially dangerous fashion. Peiping denounced the treaty for the following reasons:

1. "According to the stipulations of this treaty, the three nuclear powers may continue underground tests while the non-nuclear countries cannot conduct any nuclear tests. For, as everyone knows, the testing of nuclear weapons must begin with tests in the atmosphere. Without the data accumulated through this kind of test it would be impossible to manufacture any nuclear weapons at all."
2. "The Treaty tends to mislead the people . . . It may create an illusion among the people that U.S. imperialism loves peace. . ."
3. The Treaty aims "at binding the hands of all Socialist countries, except the Soviet Union and of all countries being oppressed by the United States, rendering it impossible for them to strengthen their defense capacity."
4. The Treaty subverts the principle of total nuclear band and general disarmament and thereby removes the basis for pressure against American imperialists for total nuclear band and general disarmament.[18]

Because of the implications of these aspects as well as of the political aspects of the nuclear test ban treaty, China felt more than ever the

[18] Cited in Chia, Hungdah, "Communist China's Attitude Towards Nuclear Tests," *The China Quarterly,* No. 21, January–March, 1965, pp. 103–104. Quotations cited are from the *Peking Review,* No. 33, 1963.

need to rely upon its own resources if it was to forge ahead. It strengthened Chinese determination to acquire its own nuclear weapons and not to be intimidated by United States nuclear superiority.

U. S. Relations with Europe

As Europe regained its strength and equilibrium, various tendencies broke through the surface to produce a major crisis in European-American relations.

Beginning in the late 1950's and with greatly increased tempo and intensity, the strategic and political dependence of Europe upon the United States began to be questioned. The Europeans' motives for questioning it are mixed. On the face of it, only France seems to question the wisdom of the existing relationship whereby the United States possesses a virtual monopoly of thermonuclear weapons. But this view overlooks the fact that the British already possess a nuclear capability and however modest it may be, it nevertheless constitutes an element of national prestige.

In fact, it is precisely in the context of Britain's special relationship to America that Britain's nuclear capability looms so large. The United States indulged the British in their desire to be a nuclear power, but it had gone out of its way to defeat any such French aspiration (at least until the Nassau conference in December 1962).

The French are convinced that no self-respecting great power can be without a nuclear deterrent. They argue that French and American interests are not necessarily the same and that nuclear subservience to the United States defeats any possibility France might have of achieving its distinctive national interests. The special relationship accorded Britain serves American interests by dividing Europe. Britain is America's instrument or better still, Trojan horse.

It is de Gaulle's contention that France must have a nuclear capability of its own in order to have an equal voice in the diplomatic and disarmament discussions between the Russians and the "Anglo-Saxons." France claims that Europe has interests that are not identical with those of the Anglo-Saxons and that so long as it stands in a relation of dependence to the Anglo-Saxons, its distinctive interests and destiny will not be realized. By developing its own striking force, de Gaulle hopes to eliminate the need for Europe's dependence on the United States and thereby assert the interests of Europe from a position of equality with the Anglo-Saxon powers. Rightly or wrongly, de Gaulle contends that America's purpose in pressing for greater military integration in NATO with reduced reliance upon nuclear weapons and a build-up of conventional forces (Secretary of Defense McNamara's strategy) is only a pretext to keep Europe dependent upon American strategy and leadership. De Gaulle's position is simply impervious to the arguments that the United States has advanced against it: that there is no need for separate allied nuclear forces; that independent forces drain resources from NATO; that independent forces tend to undermine allied cohesion; that if Britain *and* France are nuclear powers, then Germany will have to have its own nuclear force, and more diffusion of nuclear arms within the alliance would inspire more diffusion outside the alliance.[19]

These arguments are unacceptable to de Gaulle because they all justify and confirm an intolerable relationship of European dependence upon America. The French learned from the Suez crisis, when the United States refused to parry Russian threats to send nuclear rockets to London and Paris, that the United States could not be counted upon to employ its nuclear monopoly to uphold French interests if they conflicted with American interests or if America's extra non-European interests were threatened. Conversely, Europeans have become increasingly aware that the United States might feel compelled to resort to nuclear war for reasons completely unrelated to Europe. Such a war would bring the nuclear holocaust down upon Europe unless Europe possessed its own nuclear deterrent.

For these reasons France has refused to agree to the partial test ban treaty and has refused to accept missiles or nuclear stockpiles on French soil unless France is given complete control of the warheads. De Gaulle rationalizes that Britain is willing to acquiesce in the American design for NATO because the interests of the Anglo-Saxon powers are essentially the same; that because of its special relationship to America and because it possessed a nuclear capability from the beginning, the British have been permitted to remain a nuclear power and have nothing to lose through their dependence on the United States. De Gaulle also contends that without nuclear

[19] Based on Osgood, Robert, "NATO: The Entangling Alliance," in Stoessinger, J. G., and Westin, Alan F. (eds.), *Power and Order* (New York: Harcourt, Brace, 1964), pp. 66–101. A good summary of de Gaulle's views can be found in Duroselle, Jean-Baptiste, "De Gaulle's Designs for Europe and the West" in *Changing East-West Relations and the Unity of the West,* Wolfers, Arnold (ed.) (Baltimore: The Johns Hopkins Press, 1964).

power France is not listened to and that America has had sufficient failures in recent years—Cuba, Viet Nam, Laos, China—to warrant France asserting an independent voice in NATO.

It is customary for Americans to say that de Gaulle poses a threat to the future of the Common Market, the future of the already advanced movement for European unification and the future of our ancient but rapidly developing Atlantic Community.

But has the Atlantic Community been anything more than a euphemism for a common but limited security interest? As far as the movement for European unification is concerned, Great Britain consistently opposed and undercut European federation during the post-war era. The Labor Government was furious when it learned about the Schuman Plan. Churchill and Eden scoffed at EDC and would have done even more to defeat it had they thought that it had a chance of succeeding. The Common Market has succeeded in spite of British efforts to defeat it and in spite of American indifference. It was only when the continental states succeeded in making a "go" of the Common Market that London felt obliged to consider joining. Even then the conditions it set were such that they would have opened the door to other exceptions which would have been intolerable. Consequently, it is not enough to take a pious or hypocritical view of de Gaulle's rejection of an Atlantic Community that was never more than a euphemism or a European unity subject to whatever conditions and exceptions Britain would demand.

In spite of his archaic and anachronistic usages, de Gaulle's Grand Design does not represent a rejection of the Common Market. In fact, its success depends upon it. True, de Gaulle has exploited the interest which the other members have in its preservation to advance de Gaulle's own particular view of European collaboration. But in so doing, he has always recognized the stake that France has in a continental Europe linked by indissoluable bonds of economic interest and strategy.

There is of course the other inspiration of Gaullist policy; the harking back to an anachronistic French nationalism and the "tactic of saying no" and of attempting to establish French "grandeur" by taking initiatives at the expense of the United States in situations for which the United States and not France must of necessity bear the responsibility.

De Gaulle was born and bred with a fanatical, mystical attachment to the idea that France has a unique destiny. De Gaulle has written:

All my life I have thought of France in a certain way . . . as chosen for an exalted and exceptional destiny. Instinctively I have the feeling that Providence has created her either for complete successes or for exemplary misfortunes . . . France is not really herself unless she is in the front rank . . . only vast enterprises are capable of balancing the ferments of disintegration inherent in her people. . . . In short, to my mind, France cannot be France without greatness.[20]

There are several suggestive parallels between the Sino-Soviet and the Franco-American schisms. Both Mao Tse-tung and General de Gaulle suffered political set-backs at the hands of their respective partners. The interests of Chinese Communism were several times sacrificed to Soviet national interest; the interests of France appear to have been sacrificed on numerous occasions to Anglo-American interests. De Gaulle claims that the Anglo-Saxon powers let France down in 1919, again in 1938, and in 1940. They excluded France from a major role in the war and undermined her overseas empire. After 1945, they deprived France of its ambition to detach the left bank of the Rhine and the Ruhr from Germany and overrode French opinion in restoring West Germany to full military and political status. However much one may explain the record by extenuating circumstances, it is too long and too manifest to be purely coincidental. There is a gulf between France and the Anglo-Saxon powers that is far wider than the Channel. It is a psychological and political gulf which the United States has never been able to fathom nor to bridge. Without always being aware of it, England and America singly or together have spent the years since 1939 widening it.

Both China and France have been imbued with contempt for alien cultures. There is a suggestive parallel between Peiping's reputed disdain for Khrushchev's peasant heavy-handedness and Paris's less than total admiration for American culture. In a study of the French image of America written over a decade ago, the author found the most intense cultural and psychological antipathy on the part of the French toward American civilization and toward Americans as a collectivity. Beginning in the mid-1920's, French intellectuals developed an intense aversion to America reflected in most of their writings about America. Conservative writers like G. Duhamel (*Scènes de la Vie Future*) and L. Celine (*To the End of the Night*) showed themselves just as savagely anti-American as Jean Paul Sartre or Mlle. de Beauvoir (*America Day by Day*). In a terribly funda-

[20] De Gaulle, Charles, *The War Memoirs of Charles de Gaulle* (2 vols.), (New York: Simon and Schuster, 1959 & 1960).

mental way, French and Americans do not trust each other; there is an antipathy between the values of their respective civilizations that seem incapable of being transcended.

De Gaulle probably knew from the very beginning that he would orient France against America. The schism might have been mitigated had the United States been willing to treat France as a complete equal, but since that was ruled out, de Gaulle's pique has fed upon itself. In his efforts to assert France's destiny against that of both the Russians and the Anglo-Saxons, de Gaulle had very little to work with. The acquisition of a French nuclear force was obviously indispensable to any project for maximizing French diplomatic weight. The other asset was that of France's role as "leader-of-Europe." Here the Common Market which Britain and the United States had discounted and which everyone imagined de Gaulle would scuttle has proven a remarkably important instrument of French policy.

Franco-American Relations

There was already in being when Kennedy assumed the Presidency, a European Economic Community, or Common Market. Americans underestimated it because they had for so long advocated just such a type of integration without ever considering that it might assume the form of a rival. Because the Common Market was so much in line with conventional American views regarding Europe, no one had paid it particularly much attention until the balance of economic and financial power within the West suddenly began to shift to Europe. The British actively opposed the Common Market and did not expect de Gaulle, on the basis of his past antipathy to supranational organizations, to actively espouse its cause. But de Gaulle soon became aware of the virtues of the Common Market as a vehicle for his diplomacy. The Common Market had the merit of encompassing the six continental European states and constituting a natural unit with which to balance the Anglo-Saxons and the Russians. It afforded additional weight to his decisions to withhold or partially withdraw cooperation from the North Atlantic Alliance.

One of Kennedy's principal preoccupations as President was to do everything possible to minimize the destructive possibilities of nuclear war and to "put the genie of nuclear power back into the bottle." He was convinced that success in these two matters depended upon the United States retaining its unique ability to conduct "centrally controlled" nuclear war. Only if Khrushchev knew that in dealing with the United States he was dealing with the only other major possessor of nuclear capability would it be possible to get nuclear control. Kennedy believed that an important condition of such agreement would be to minimize the proliferation of nuclear power. But to do that Kennedy would have to deny France the very thing that de Gaulle had set as the sine qua non of continued Atlantic partnership. As is so often true of international politics, one goal can only be advanced at the sacrifice of another. The main thrust of United States policy after 1961 was opposed to sharing nuclear responsibility with Europe, exacerbating de Gaulle's suspicion that the United States was seeking a worldwide détente with Russia at the expense of France and Europe.

Kennedy and de Gaulle had met in Paris in June 1961 and agreed to meet twice a year and "to get together once more before the year was out."[21] The two leaders never met again. By the time the year was out, the patterns of French and American policies had begun to set along antagonistic lines. The Kennedy Administration's Grand Design, which was unveiled toward the end of 1961, looked suspiciously like an American design to box de Gaulle (as did the MLF a year later).

Disagreement continued to attend their respective attitudes toward Khrushchev's pressure at Berlin. Kennedy remained convinced that there was a danger of war through miscalculation at Berlin. De Gaulle was convinced that Kennedy and Rusk did not understand Khrushchev's character and motives. Adenauer, who for obvious reasons did not want to negotiate at all and mistrusted the Anglo-American position, gravitated to de Gaulle. Adenauer's position reinforced de Gaulle's propensity to play upon the theme that the United States was seeking a worldwide détente with Russia at the expense of Germany and Europe. The Kennedy Administration deeply resented this interpretation. For these reasons Secretary of State Dean Rusk argued that nuclear sharing with France would not overcome the basic animus of de Gaulle's statecraft against the United States or make France more cooperative: "de Gaulle's conflicts with the U.S and NATO, which were essentially political, could not be resolved that way."[22] Rusk ostensibly based his opposition to nuclear sharing on the ground that "proliferation of nuclear weapons would be stimulated and that Germany would become the next claimant, provoking a dangerous Russian response."[23]

21 Kleiman, Robert, *Atlantic Crisis* (New York: W. W. Norton, 1964), p. 38.
22 *Ibid.*, p. 56.
23 *Ibid.*, p. 57.

If Rusk's position reflects a genuine consideration and not just pique at de Gaulle's pretentiousness, it is a striking commentary on the importance that a nuclear arms deal with the Soviet Union had assumed in Kennedy's policy. The issue of central control vs. proliferation was further complicated by Kennedy's call for the creation of a Multilateral Nuclear Force, a mixed, manned NATO missile fleet.

The result of Kennedy's diplomacy at the time was to throw Adenauer and de Gaulle together and to give greater substance than ever to de Gaulle's argument that Europe had a destiny distinct from that of the United States. Franco-German relations began to crystallize into a common set of attitudes.

An almost inevitable outcome of the new alignment within the Atlantic Community was to reinforce the divisive tendencies. Kennedy felt that he could no longer make headway with de Gaulle so he ceased talking to him. By contrast Kennedy "found that he could talk with Macmillan . . . without compromising the Kennedy concept of American leadership."[24] As Rusk explained it later: "We can't break with Britain. We have to be able to discuss world problems with someone. We can't discuss them with de Gaulle. . . . We and the British don't always agree. But we discuss."[25]

Adenauer, by contrast, felt more and more at home with de Gaulle's projects. The unsatisfactory diplomatic situation within the Atlantic Community gave impetus to the Common Market with de Gaulle making concessions to seal German loyalty, concessions which he would not normally have made so readily.

By the spring of 1962, de Gaulle was supremely confident that with Adenauer committed, he could openly flaunt his own Grand Design. On May 15, 1962, de Gaulle restated the essential elements of his vision of Europe. What he saw was a Union of European States, fairly flexible in its operations, whose heads of state or government, meeting periodically, would make the really important decisions. De Gaulle took pleasure in noting that such a confederal structure would be far more likely to appeal to Great Britain than a more organic one.[26]

Only the previous winter McGeorge Bundy had unveiled the Kennedy Administration's plan for the North Atlantic community. In a widely publicized speech of December 6, 1961, Bundy attempted to scotch the Gaullist argument that the United States was only inter-

[24] *Ibid.*, p. 44.
[25] *Ibid.*, p. 55.
[26] *The New York Times,* May 16, 1962, p. 1.

ested in a Europe too weak and divided to threaten United States leadership. The only productive way of conceiving the political future of the Atlantic Community, Bundy declared, "is to think in terms of a partnership between the United States, on the one hand, and a great European power, on the other. . . . It would not be an ingrown white man's club; it would rather look outward to larger burdens and opportunities."[27] President Kennedy followed this up with an Independence Day speech in 1962 calling for "interdependence" between a United Europe and a United States.[28]

In a concerted effort to make good on his offer of "partnership" to Europe and to offset the pull that Paris was exerting on Bonn, the Kennedy Administration began actively promoting the concept of the Multilateral Nuclear Force.

MLF met two requirements for American policy. It could be effectively argued against Soviet objections that it did not constitute a net proliferation of nuclear weapons or a loss of centrally directed control. At the same time it gave the Europeans and especially the West Germans a new stake in NATO, that of sharing directly on an equal basis with the other NATO partners in control of nuclear weapons. Two years later MLF was shelved, but at the time it did yeoman service in tying West Germany to NATO.

It is unfortunate that the United States did not simply consent to the French acquisition of a purely French "force de frappe" while utilizing MLF "to give Germany a participating role with the United States in the joint management of nuclear weapons. . ."[29] Instead, the United States appeared to promote the accession of the other European states to a nuclear status through MLF as a means of isolating France. The United States came perilously close to staking the existence of NATO upon its ability to "break" France. De Gaulle could have asked for nothing better. "To be great," he wrote in an early memoir, *Le Fil de l'Epée,* "is to sustain a great quarrel."

Britain and the Common Market

Under these circumstances, Britain's procrastinations and efforts to gain admission to the Common Market on strictly British terms were viewed coldly. Having discovered the potency of Franco-German

[27] Address to the Economic Club of Chicago, December 6, 1961. *The New York Times,* December 7, 1961.

[28] *The New York Times,* July 5, 1962, p. 1.

[29] Osgood, Robert E., *The Case for the MLF: A Critical Evaluation,* published under the auspices of The Washington Center of Foreign Policy Research, 1964, p. 50.

collaboration, de Gaulle had no intention of letting Britain dilute or weaken its political value. Britain had too much the character of a stalking horse or, as de Gaulle called it, Trojan Horse, with which Kennedy would, if he could, undermine the Paris-Bonn axis. Rightly or wrongly, Britain's efforts to enter the Common Market on special terms only lent credence to de Gaulle's suspicion.

After a year of painful negotiations, Macmillan and de Gaulle met at the Chateau de Champs on June 2 and 3, 1962, where it was understood that upon satisfactory completion of the negotiations, Britain would come into the Common Market. As late as August or September or even October, British entry was still possible. By November when de Gaulle and Macmillan met again, it was already too late. Why? Partly because of continued British procrastination. But partly also because of a radical strengthening of de Gaulle's position—both domestic and foreign. Contrary to his own expectation, the Union for the New Republic and other Gaullists captured 32 per cent of the popular vote in the November elections, which together with the Independents, gave de Gaulle's government an absolute majority in the Assembly. Among the other Common Market countries dissatisfaction was growing over Britain's dilatory tactics. It became known that Macmillan, far from being ready to sign, preferred to hold elections after which the British Government would make the necessary concessions to complete the agreement. Meanwhile, the British were holding up implementation of France's hard-won Common Market agriculture policy as well as other French projects. Although de Gaulle did not reveal his hand at the time, by the time his meetings with Macmillan in December took place, just before the Nassau Conference, de Gaulle appears to have made up his mind that he could safely veto Britain's admission.

When Macmillan met with de Gaulle at the Chateau de Rambouillet en route to his meeting four days later with Kennedy at Nassau, his policies only served to convince de Gaulle that Britain's negotiations for admission to the Common Market had to be broken off. On the one hand, Macmillan again repeated that the British were ready to work for political union, including a common defense policy. But on the other hand he gave every indication that he was determined to secure a satisfactory nuclear weapons system for Britain even if it meant continuing Britain's relationship of dependency upon the United States. This was precisely the sort of ambiguity about Britain's position that European federationists were willing to overlook but that did not meet de Gaulle's idea of a Europe acting upon strictly European motives.

There was no room in de Gaulle's view of the Common Market for a relationship of dependency upon the United States, which in principle might extend to 1980. The purpose of the Common Market was essentially political to de Gaulle's way of thinking; it was to be the means by which Europe would assert its demand for a fully equal partnership within the North Atlantic Community. Because it was precisely Europe's state of nuclear dependency upon America that lay at the root of its inferiority, Macmillan's eager pursuit of a new American missile system was fundamentally incompatible with de Gaulle's plans for the Common Market.

Meanwhile, the findings of the efficiency experts in the Pentagon were fashioning a fuse that would blow North Atlantic relations to smithereens. Three years earlier, the British for financial reasons had abandoned development of their medium-range ballistic missile, Blue Streak. Eisenhower had agreed that Britain could buy Skybolt, an American missile capable of being launched from a bomber, with a range of 1,000 miles. Now it was discovered that Skybolt was too expensive for whatever additional margin of security it promised; McNamara had persuaded Kennedy to agree to drop it from production. Macmillan was left without a British deterrent, an unpleasant predicament for a Conservative leader facing an election. McNamara next informed the British that the United States "would be prepared to sell the submarine-launched missiles to Britain,"[30] but only if Britain committed its Polaris submarine force "irrevocably" to NATO. This is the situation that prevailed when Kennedy and Macmillan met at Nassau in December, 1962.

At Nassau, Kennedy agreed to provide British subs with Polaris missiles in return for a British agreement to commit its deterrent to NATO. The same offer was to be made to de Gaulle. By getting Macmillan to agree to commit Britain's formerly "independent" deterrent to NATO, Kennedy opened the way to offering France equal treatment without accepting the concept of a completely independent nuclear force. The Nassau transaction promised to put Britain and France on an equal footing without sacrificing the principle of central control of all nuclear forces. Had Kennedy and Macmillan gone directly to Paris and made the gist of the offer directly to de Gaulle, they might have succeeded in persuading him that the American offer was being made "not to Britain, but to an integrated European nuclear force based on a joint Anglo-French effort open to others."[31]

[30] Kleiman, *op. cit.*, p. 54.
[31] *Ibid.*, p. 61.

Unfortunately, by not doing this and by announcing the decision from Nassau, Kennedy lent credence to the image of an Anglo-Saxon deal; Britain had seemingly obtained with ease privileged treatment at Nassau, thus providing the French with an excellent pretext to make a complete break with them. In his semiannual press conference on January 14, 1963, de Gaulle announced to eight hundred journalists: "L'angleterre n'a pas la possibilité d'entrés." [Entry to the Common Market is not open to Britain].

The historic schism between Britain and the Continent was reaffirmed—at least for President de Gaulle's lifetime. It is doubtful if any other decision would have been forthcoming even had the Nassau offer been extended to de Gaulle. Having already made up his mind to veto Britain's admission to the Common Market, he could scarcely have opened nuclear negotiations with the United States.

The reasoning behind de Gaulle's decision was his long-standing conviction that the Cold War developed out of a purely transient situation of bipolarity and then became reinforced by ideological passion. An Atlantic Alliance dominated by the United States could only prolong the ideological confrontation and inhibit a return to a more normal set of relationships. Therefore, it is both good for peace and good for Europe to refuse to remain any longer subordinate to United States control. He reminded his audience that the six Common Market countries were so unified because none of them had outside ties of special political or military agreement. After examining the hypothesis of Britain's admission he concluded:

> It is conceivable that the cohesion of the many and most diverse members of an enlarged Community will not long endure and that, in the final analysis, there will appear a colossal Atlantic Community dependent on, and directed by, America and which would soon absorb the European Community. This is a hypothesis that can be perfectly well justified to some, but it is not what France wanted to do nor what she is doing, which is the development of a European structure properly so called.[32]

The New Europe

Up to a point, the economic benefits that have been realized from the Common Market by its six members are very real, especially for West Germany. But there is still no common political authority without which a common foreign policy and strategic effort are

[32] *The New York Times,* January 15, 1963.

unattainable. And de Gaulle has never indicated that he intended to submerge French sovereignty in a supranational European political authority. Speaking of the existing economic institutions de Gaulle has declared:

Admittedly as a provisional measure, we have been able to set up a number of more or less supra-national bodies; these bodies have their technical value but they have not, and cannot have, any political authority. . . . As long as nothing serious happens, they function fairly well without too much trouble, but as soon as something dramatic happens and a serious problem has to be settled, it can be seen that no High Authority has political authority: it is only states which have it.[33]

Although the potential exists to develop a politically integrated Europe, which has been all along the goal of European federalists, this kind of union has not been de Gaulle's plan. De Gaulle is primarily interested in the Common Market and the European community as a means of averting a "colossal Atlantic community" dominated by the United States and he has made it abundantly clear that he values European integration only so far as it is essential to Europe's becoming a "third force" dominated by France, independent of the Anglo-Saxons, and able to pursue policies independently of both Russia and the United States. Most of the advances that France has executed in the Common Market were taken only when de Gaulle felt these steps to be in the national—rather than the European—interest.

"The Gaullist vision of the New Europe is neither supra-national nor federal. It is confederal; it limits the participants to ministers, the contexts to the political in the grand sense and the quality of the decisions to unanimous agreements defined by the leading nations."[34]

Logically there are severe limits to de Gaulle's design. The West Germans will not be content indefinitely to play second fiddle to de Gaulle, although an important rightist and nationalist strain led by Franz Joseph Strauss, for the time being, strongly advocates strengthening Germany's ties with Paris at the expense of Washington. But most Germans are still convinced that only the United States can guarantee Berlin and only the United States has sufficient stake in maintaining a policy of nonrecognition of East Germany. For Western Europe to have a credible nuclear foreign policy in its own right it will have to be as unified and monolithic as the United

[33] *France and the European Economic Unity,* (PEP pamphlet) January 1961, p. 10.

[34] Haas, *op. cit.,* p. 72.

States or the Soviet Union. A confederal approach does not fulfill this condition. When the present Gaullist interregnum is over, Europe will have the choice between remaining essentially a civilization of nation-states strengthened economically by a Common Market or it can take up the advance toward complete economic and political union. But in either case, it seems apparent that relations with the United States will have to be on the basis of genuine partnership. The European's sense of confidence in his civilization has been remarkably restored since 1945. Although it is true that America's nuclear strategy will remain the ultimate guarantee of their security, the Europeans together or singly will no longer settle for a relationship of dependence. The danger is that unless the Europeans develop a large enough stake in the Common Market, they may end up being divided by other national interests. The United States has for too long asked the Europeans, especially the French, to postpone their demands for a political adjustment of relations in the name of abstract considerations of nuclear strategy and East-West diplomacy. De Gaulle is going out of his way to demonstrate that European nationalism can no longer be disregarded. But he has no answer for German nationalism or the German desire to be reunited. It would be unwise for the United States to attempt to exploit the potential of Franco-German rivalry already evident in Germany's eager support for MLF. To do so would be to play Moscow's game completely. The best course would be to attempt to bear with de Gaulle and work with the genuine Europeanists in both countries, in anticipation of the day when, de Gaulle gone from the scene, a fully effective partnership can be restored. Europe with its strategic position and the wealth and genius of its people is still the pivot of world power, still the prize sought by Soviet diplomacy.

In a sense, although de Gaulle's premodern view of the primacy of national sovereignty and a *politique de grandeur* is obstructing European integration and defeating American leadership and strategy, it may not outlive its progenitor. The forces of economic integration are continuing and those of political integration will eventually be strengthened by the economic knitting and binding together that is presently occurring. However, it would be a mistake to believe that Europe will revert to the status of dependence on the United States that it assumed from 1947 to 1960.

For the first time, the impetus to examine European-American relations is coming not from the external threat of the Soviet Union, but from concern with an internal conflict. Even without de Gaulle, the Common Market countries would have begun to assert a challenge and a demand for genuine partnership. As the high tide of Soviet-American tensions began to recede, it inevitably revealed the shoals and headlands that separate European and American positions on certain critical issues. There will be less incentive in the future for Europe to overlook these distinctions of interest. Europe, including Germany, may be tempted to do more and more bargaining on its own, playing upon interests that the members of the Eastern bloc may have in a détente. There will be no real settlement in Central Europe as long as Germany remains divided. Yet Russia cannot afford to recognize a change in the status quo that would weaken its relative power position and capacity to control its security in Eastern Europe. The most likely prospects are for the growth of economic relations which, together with the general détente, would mitigate the acuteness of rivalry, insecurity, and tension in Central Europe.

In summary, the crisis within the North Atlantic Alliance that came to the fore under Kennedy was due to the multiplying number of issues upon which it was difficult to achieve agreement. During the 1950's, the quest for independence by the colonial peoples and the differing interests and assessments of the legitimacy of those independence movements added a divisive factor to the Alliance. During the 1960's, differences among the British, French, Americans, and Germans on the priority and degree of risk to be run to alter the status quo regarding East Germany added yet another divisive factor. Finally, the degree of reliance to be placed upon America's nuclear deterrent in the light of Soviet advances in weapons technology and ICBM's provided President de Gaulle with an excuse to develop an independent deterrent, thereby dividing the Alliance even further. Whatever happens to the Common Market, whether Europe becomes united or remains a collection of sovereign states, its relationship within the Alliance will be either a partnership or national rivals.

Relations with the Third World

The struggle between the United States and the Soviet Union may have turned into a deadlock in which each side has "bloc" problems and each has strong incentives to retrench and concentrate on domestic problems. But historical processes cannot be rescheduled. Scores of new nation-states had come into being by 1961 but their revolutionary impact on world politics seems barely to have begun. The world into which the new states are emerging is one largely of Western creation, and it is one that the new states are bound to want to change. The controlling mood in some of these states is aggressive and xenophobic (Egypt) and in some, hysterical and destructive (Indonesia). Everywhere these new nations are obsessed by anticolonialism and hence anti-Westernism. In a sense, anticolonialism continues to be a substitute for a nonexistent or only partially established spirit of national unity and purpose. Furthermore, theirs is a resentment that is bound to be intensified by the growing sense of frustration with their inferior and hopeless economic and social status.

When Kennedy took over, the full impact of the forces in motion in the "third world" was beginning to be felt on a rapidly rising scale. Castro was veering toward the Communist camp at an accelerated rate; the French war in Algeria was at its peak and a critical situation existed in the Congo, both of which situations tended to divide the African nations against the European powers; and the long smoldering subversionary war in Laos and Viet Nam was becoming incendiary.

All three situations—Cuba, Congo, Southeast Asia—were harbingers and symptoms of another critical phase in world relations. Castroism held out an appeal to the submerged and turbulent masses of Latin America to overthrow the existing status quo and embark upon an economic and social revolution. The collapse of government in the Congo was simply an extreme example of the crisis facing most of the newly independent African states: the disintegrative effects of regional and tribal differences, combined with economic and political inexperience, to produce chaos. Under the circumstances, the leadership feels it is imperative to set up repressive one-party rule with themselves as venerated figures or to indulge in wars with their neighbors to unify or divert popular opinion. Examples of these conflicts are Algeria vs. Morocco, Ethiopia vs. Somalia, Egypt vs. Saudi-backed forces in Yemen, Iraq vs. Kuwait, and of course, India vs. Pakistan and Indonesia vs. Malaysia.

In all three areas, the revolution was being transmitted neither by the Red Army as had been the case in Eastern Europe, nor by direct aggression, as had been the case in Korea, but by the subtle application of violence under politically favorable circumstances, which renders it all the more intractable and difficult to handle. In all three areas, the Communists were exploiting the inevitable forces of nationalism and anti-imperialism (in Cuba anti-neocolonialism) and utilizing methods that defied Western military power or control.

The United States in all these areas must decide how to preserve and sustain the viability of various local non-Communist governments without appearing to be interfering, either by embroiling them in the Cold War or by strengthening one at the expense of another. Domestic and interstate relations in all these areas are so fragile and volatile that America's presence can just as easily provoke instability as sustain stability, as we learned in the 1950's. The lessons were clear in America's ill-starred interventions in the Middle East and in South Asia, in which we extended military aid to Pakistan and thereby worsened relations with India. But it is not so clear that we learned the lesson well enough.

Castroism and Latin America

The sudden eruption of Castro onto the Cuban scene put United States policy in Latin America to an extreme test. United States policy in Latin America during the 1950's had been conceived in security terms and consisted of military missions and equipment and the signing of Mutual Defense Agreements. In purely military terms the pacts were useless—Latin America could hardly become a field of armed conflict without United States power being decisive—it was therefore highly questionable whether military aid was the best instrument to secure general political support.

Latin American scholars generally agree that United States military assistance has contributed to strengthening the military at the expense of the civilian and middle class sectors.

> It is difficult to escape the conclusion that it [U.S. military aid] is a contributory cause of militarism in Latin America. Further, that the shift in emphasis from hemispheric security to internal security capabilities will make the Latin American military better trained and equipped than ever to intervene in the political systems of their nations. This may be the hidden price tag on the anticommunist security which the United States seeks in the Western Hemisphere through the MAP.[35]

In many instances the arms merely served to entrench lackluster dictatorships. Instead of avoiding collaboration with the more reactionary and antisocial forces in Latin America, the United States seemed to go out of its way to court them, thereby feeding popular anti-Yankee sentiment. The opposition forces are usually made up of various political elements; our military aid has had the effect of

[35] Powell, John Duncan, "Military Assistance and Militarism in Latin America," *The Western Political Quarterly,* Vol. XVIII, No. 2, Part 1, June 1965, p. 388.

estranging them from us and driving them in directions susceptible to Communist influence.

The sudden deterioration in the terms of trade of the Latin-American countries after the Korean War combined with the population explosion added economic stagnation and inflation to political instability. Some adjustments in American policy to meet the critical nature of the situation had occurred even before Eisenhower left office, but they were hardly commensurate with the magnitude of the problems. Disturbed by the fear that Latin America might "blow up" and open the way to Communism, the Eisenhower Administration had sharply increased the amount of credit available to Latin American public and private institutions for development purposes; but this credit was never enough and was always subject to stringent terms. Kennedy gave dramatic new impetus to Latin American affairs with the Alliance for Progress, established by the Charter of Punta del Este, on August 17, 1961.

The philosophy of the Alliance was clear and simple:

> The U.S. must appear as a free society supporting free societies ready to help themselves; only thus could it appear as the champion of a better way of life than that modelled in the Soviet bloc. It must therefore see that aid went to "progressive" democracies.[36]

The implication that the United States would henceforth discriminate between democratic reformist regimes and traditional military or oligarchic dictatorships was a striking departure from the pattern of the previous decade. On his visits to Colombia and Venezuela, Kennedy publicly challenged the Latin American governments to embark upon a program of land reform leading to social and economic progress. The Kennedy administration actively supported the Presidency of Juan Bosch, successor to the Dominican Republic's military strong man General Rafael Trujillo although it failed to back him when he was overthrown in 1963.

Unfortunately, the political, social, and economic conditions in Latin America are not conducive to the straightforward operation of a developmental process powered by American aid plus private investment. The obstacles are truly enormous. Latin American countries are still primarily dependent upon the export of raw materials for their balance of payments. They are at the mercy of adverse terms of trade and of fluctuations in demand among the advanced indus-

[36] Carr, Ray, "Latin America," in *The Cold War,* Evan Luard (ed.) (New York: Praeger, 1964), p. 233.

trial countries. Latin America's trade position reflects the predominance of an almost feudal agrarian system in many countries beset by deep societal handicaps to economic development. Sweeping and fundamental agrarian reform would only constitute a beginning; much wider economic and social reforms would also be needed. The feudal economic and social mores characteristic of the agrarian sector of the economy carry over into the urban and industrial sectors and, together with the political control that the vested interests possess, successfully inhibits and defeats the conditions essential to orderly economic growth and modernization. The result is a vicious circle in which chaotic and explosive forces build up but find no effective outlet.

The Alliance for Progress, grandiose in scope and conception—calling for the investment of some $100 billion over a ten year period, $20 billion in the form of United States government grants and loans and $80 billion in private investment—could hardly be expected to transform the economic and social condition of Latin America overnight. In practice the Alliance could expect to accomplish little more than remedy the impression of neglect and ameliorate certain of the worst social and economic evils and imbalances. Only revolution, if anything, can radically reform Latin America, and the United States is not in a position to foster revolutions. The Alliance for Progress represented a distinct advance over previous American approaches, but its effectiveness is still uncertain. While working for social and economic reform the United States does not intend to let another Castroite regime come to power if it can help it.

The ill-considered and ill-starred attempt to overthrow Castro was in line with the older, more traditional methods; so was the intervention in the Dominican Republic. No great power is likely to be dissuaded from acting if it believes its vital interests are at stake and it has the power to do something about it. Being unwilling to intervene directly in Cuba the United States might better have limited itself to diplomatic and political moves to isolate Castroism.

This catastrophic failure of the Bay of Pigs immediately restored both Castro's sagging domestic position and his strength throughout Latin America. Kennedy only added to his miseries when at the second meeting of the Alliance for Progress, the United States government attempted to have Cuba ostracized and an embargo instituted against Castro on the grounds that Castroism represented aggression under the Rio de Janeiro Treaty of 1947. The big four of Latin America—Mexico, Brazil, Argentina, and Chile—refused to endorse the United States policy. They constituted a bloc opposed to any attempt by the United States to interfere with the internal regime of any member state of the Organization of American States, even on the grounds that Castroism constituted an alien force threatening the security of the Western hemisphere.

As a result the United States may have dissipated a good deal of the energy and good will that had been mobilized by the initial launching of the *Alianza*. In Latin America as elsewhere, the dilemma of American policy is twofold. The kinds of reforms and growth needed in Latin America can only come about quickly if there is fundamental, virtually revolutionary land and fiscal reforms. But these are the kinds that threaten the conservative business and military interests which, playing upon this country's security consciousness, arouse American fears.

The Communist bloc is clearly counting upon revolutionary developments in the Afro-Asian and the Latin American world to overwhelm the United States. Chinese Communist global strategy holds that revolutionary bases must be established in the rural areas (the third world) so that the cities (the United States and Western Europe) can be encircled and overthrown. According to Marshal Lin Piao, China's Minister of Defense: "In the final analysis, the whole cause of world revolution hinges on the revolutionary struggles of the Asian, African, and Latin-American peoples . . . The Socialist countries should regard it as their internationalist duty to support the people's revolutionary struggle . . ." The Communist bloc is clearly counting upon these "historically inevitable" confrontations between "neocolonialism" and the surging demands of the backward and exploited peoples to engender hasty and unwise reactions on America's part. The degree to which the United States loses control of its emotions and resorts to repressive behavior will strengthen Communist strategy.

Congo Crisis and Africa

Kennedy's policy in Africa took a somewhat different approach. As a power with worldwide interests but only limited capabilities, the United States has long relied upon the United Nations to provide a second set "of mechanisms by means of which national actions could in some degree be controlled, harmonized, and channeled for the common benefit."[37] The days of assuming that there was an automatic harmony between United States policy and United Nations policy

[37] Stebbins, R., *United States in World Affairs: 1961*, (New York: Vintage, 1962), p. 345.

were long since past. Ever since the United States embarked upon alliance diplomacy to supplement the defunct collective security arrangements under the United Nations it has had to steer a delicate course between its commitments to its allies and its commitments to the United Nations. The greatest dilemma posed for the United States in this regard has been that of choosing between the interests of one's allies as colonial powers and the aspirations of the Afro-Asians for independence. In this regard, no matter how circumspect its voting record has been, the United States had had to risk the displeasure of its allies in order not to appear to oppose the numerous Afro-Asian peoples.

In a revolutionary world the United Nations offers a means for imposing some kind of order, however rudimentary, and of mobilizing world opinion through the commitment, however fragile, which many peoples and their governments feel toward the United Nations.

> A reputation for dedication to such a system [as the United Nations] and for leadership in its operation has become an asset that the United States could forego only at a high cost in terms of appeal to foreign peoples and also of public support for its foreign policy at home.[38]

Knowing the sentiments of the African nations against the renewal of white intrusion into Africa, the United States made support of the United Nations the basis of its policy in the Congo. Deeply conscious of the limitations of its power to cope with trouble on the vast African continent and keenly aware of America's susceptibility to charges of racism and neocolonialism, the United States has wisely tried to insulate Africa from the Cold War. The first serious test of this policy came in the Congo in 1960–1961. In the wake of Belgium's precipitate decision to accord independence to its African colony, the new Congo nation fell into a state of anarchy. In the struggle to restore order in the Congo and prevent the outbreak of civil war and foreign intervention, the United States gave full and unstinting backing to the United Nations and to its energetic Secretary-General Dag Hammarskjold. The United Nations task was complicated by the existence of rival factions, one of which was led by Moise Tshombé, leader of the Congolese province of Katanga, the seat of rich European mining operations. To most African leaders and of course to the Communist bloc countries, Tshombé's overt opposition to the central Congolese government was nothing but the instrument of European imperialism masking under new forms.

[38] Wolfers, Arnold, *Alliance Policy in the Cold War* (Baltimore: Johns Hopkins, 1959), p. 67.

The United Nations operation to preserve the existence and rebuild the Congo state flowed from two sources of authority, one the following resolution in which the Security Council decided

> . . . to authorize the Secretary General to take the necessary steps, in consultation with the Government of the Republic of the Congo, to provide the Government with such military assistance as may be necessary, until, through the efforts of the Congolese Government with the technical assistance of the United Nations, the national security forces may be able, in the opinion of the Government, to meet fully their tasks.[39]

The other source of authority for many of the actions taken in the course of the Congo peacekeeping operation was the Secretary General himself. Hammarskjold stretched his competence almost to the breaking point by making decisions and initiating actions that would normally have been taken only after extensive debates and votes. By the end of 1960 and beginning of 1961, the United Nations was virtually governing the strife-torn Republic and certainly providing it with the means—both civilian and military—that alone kept it afloat.

In the course of these operations, which were complicated by the deposition and political murder of the Congo's first Prime Minister, Patrice Lumumba, and by the refusal of Tshombé to accept the authority of the Central Government, Soviet influence was excluded from the country. The other African states became severely divided over the question of whether the United Nations was acting with sufficient regard for the sovereignty of the Congo and the integrity of the Congolese people.

These circumstances gave the Soviet Union the opportunity to press home its attack upon the United Nations operation. As early as July 21, 1960, the Soviet Union lodged the caveat that it did not regard the Security Council's initial resolution "as endowing the United Nations with the right to interfere in the domestic affairs of a state and to assume responsibility for a country's domestic laws and regulations."[40]

A month later V. V. Kuznetsov, First Deputy Minister of Foreign Affairs of the USSR, attacked the United Nations plan as a "limitation of the sovereignty of the Republic of the Congo," and also attacked the preponderance of Westerners on the ONUC Civilian Operations' Staff. "The implementation of the proposed plan," Kuznetsov charged, "would mean that the development of the Congo

[39] U. N. Document S/4387.

[40] Security Council Records, 879th Meeting, 21 July 1960, p. 24.

would be conducted along lines satisfactory to the United States, and this might in fact not only jeopardize the independence of the Republic of the Congo but also create a dangerous precedent for the future."[41] "A more fundamental issue, though, was really at stake. The core of the Soviet position was that state-preserving and state-building were not and could not be treated as apolitical tasks."[42] From the Soviet point of view, Hammarskjold was vastly exceeding his power when he authorized operations of the character being undertaken to preserve order in the Congo, without approval of the Security Council.

The results were just as Kuznetsov had warned. The United Nations Congo Operation did run very much parallel to American policy lines for Africa. As a result, both the Soviet bloc and the residual imperialist interests within the European states objected violently. De Gaulle joined the Soviet Union in protesting the United Nations actions and in refusing to pay their share of the costs of the operation. In a news conference on April 11, 1961 the French leader declared that France "does not wish to contribute her men or her money to any present or eventual undertaking of this organization —or disorganization."[43]

Khrushchev went a step farther. "Infuriated by the manner in which Secretary Hammarskjold had interpreted his responsibilities in the Congo, the USSR had devised a plan which, if adopted, would make it impossible for the United Nations ever again to take an action opposed by the Soviet Government. Instead of a single Secretary-General, the Khrushchev plan provided for a three-man executive made up of representatives of the 'Western,' 'socialist,' and 'neutral' countries, all three of whom would have to act in agreement if they were to act at all."[44] This so-called "troika" plan won little support outside the Communist bloc, but it represented an effort to weaken the United Nations by appealing to the resentments and aspirations that many of the new nations felt for a bigger role. For all of Khrushchev's bluster against the "domination" exercised by a particular group of "imperialist states" and for all his table thumping, he proved unable to secure any sweeping modification of the United Nations structure.

[41] U. N. Document S/4446, p. 2.

[42] Jacobson, H. D., "ONUC's Civilian Operations," *World Politics,* October 1964, p. 88.

[43] Stebbins, *op. cit.,* 347.

[44] *Ibid.,* p. 348.

While the United States was sympathetic to Hammarskjold's efforts to make the United Nations "a dynamic instrument of government" as opposed to a "static conference machinery," the basic problem of the Soviet veto remained as omnipresent as ever. Furthermore, the growing number of new states that were eager to use the United Nations as an instrument to break up the last remnants of colonialism and racism in South Africa and in Portugal's African colonies were unwilling to take the same interest and responsibility for such acute problems as those of Berlin or Southeast Asia. Nevertheless the very fact that the United Nations was able to act at all in the Congo indicates that it has an unexpected potential that the United States might well consider developing for use elsewhere. Instead of promoting United Nations strength, the United States paralyzed the U.N. for over a year by making an issue under Article 19 of Russia's and France's failure to pay their share of peacekeeping operations. The United States reasoned that unless all members are willing to pay the costs of special peacekeeping operations, others will follow the example of Russia and France, and the United Nations will become paralyzed anyway. In August 1965, President Johnson wisely reversed American opposition to France's and Russia's right to vote in the General Assembly rather than risk collapse of the U.N.

Laos and Viet Nam

Laos and Viet Nam afford prime examples of a type of situation that may become increasingly common in the world. There the conditions have proven almost perfect for the development of revolutionary subversion—a fusing of nationalism and Communism in the form of guerrilla warfare.

In Viet Nam the United States is experiencing first-hand the devastating consequences that occur when ideology and terror are unleashed within an underdeveloped society devoid of a unifying spirit of nationalism and without an effective apparatus of state power. Whether the Viet Cong is sponsored by North Viet Nam or primarily indigenous to South Viet Nam, the struggle has become essentially political; the disintegrative force is not an army but an idea in the heads of thousands of individuals organized and controlled as guerrillas.

When the United States stepped blithely into France's place in Viet Nam and Laos in 1955 it remembered Korea. There, once the Communists had been shown that America intended to defend the area against aggression, a modus vivendi had been achieved. In Viet Nam we were determined to avoid the necessity of demonstrating our determination by registering our presence immediately. But a number of differences existed between the Korean and Vietnamese situations: one was a peninsula, easily defensible; the other a long slice of territory contiguous to Communist and neutralist borders but joined by a vast sea of jungle and grassland. Furthermore, the South Koreans were unified by a tough nationalism ingrained by centuries of struggle to survive between the Chinese and the Japanese; South Viet Nam suffers all the divisions so characteristic of the countries of Southeast Asia: different peoples at different stages of economic development, acute religious differences, and an almost total absence of a strong sense of nationalism to offset one's loyalty to family, tribe, or clan. The United States had taken an active role in the affairs of both Laos and South Viet Nam and refused to honor the principle of neutralization because it feared a settlement unfavorable to the independence of those two countries. "The advent of the Kennedy Administration brought with it a more definite acceptance of 'neutrality' and 'independence' as the proper status for Laos,"[45] and negotiations with Moscow and London led to an uneasy neutralization of the country on the basis of spheres of influence. It is doubtful that such neutralization can ever succeed unless there is a strong indigenous force to back it up and some means of making it worth the while of neighboring states not to violate the neutrality.

The same course was not adopted in South Viet Nam. There the obvious pro-American character of the government and its importance to the general intention that the United States wished to convey of determination to remain a power in Southeast Asia made the threats to its existence unacceptable.

Consequently Kennedy, lacking any other means of making credible America's determination to maintain South Viet Nam free of Communist domination, accepted President Diem's invitation to send in American civilian and military advisers in 1961 to help in logistics and communications functions and to train and advise the Vietnamese army. The American intervention was accompanied by two developments of disturbing import: the guerrilla Viet Cong began to step up its activities and influential persons close to President Diem began to resent American pressures for social and administrative reform. Caught between the millstones of Viet Cong terror and

[45] *Ibid.*, p. 195.

stepped-up American pressure for action, the always fragile Vietnamese society began to crumble. In a sense, the more the American government substituted its efforts for those of the Viet Nam government, the more a sense of artificiality, illusion, and hideous make-believe crept into South Vietnamese life and affairs. It was all grist to the Viet Cong mills as Viet Nam was swept swiftly toward destruction. It can be argued that the United States policy in Viet Nam failed because both the United States and the Diem regime lacked sufficient will and discipline to do what was necessary to make defense of the populace against the guerrillas possible.

Neither the genius of American technology and military strategy nor the suffering of the Vietnamese people seemed able to redeem the situation. The inevitable dialectics of political terror defied all efforts to stabilize South Viet Nam. The longer the war continued the more it appeared that the United States was supporting a Saigon puppet against the interests of the Vietnamese people. The American government believes that it has no choice but to meet the challenge of violent change promoted under the aegis of "liberation movements."

The End of the Sino-Soviet Alliance

From its very beginning the Sino-Soviet dispute has been marked by a depth of bitterness that we associate with religious wars. Moscow has branded the Chinese as "Trotskyite adventurers" and Peiping denounces the leadership in Moscow as "class collaborators" (i.e., in collaboration with the American imperialists) and "revisionists." After 1960 the ideological struggle between Moscow and Peiping began a rapid escalation as each vied for leadership of the movement. As long as Soviet-American relations deteriorated over Berlin and Cuba, the Chinese may still have entertained hopes of Sino-Soviet reconciliation. Nevertheless Peiping was now determined to assert Chinese national interests come what may. Taking advantage of an ill-considered Indian attempt to dislodge them from a disputed strip in the North East Frontier area of India, the Chinese army delivered India a shattering military blow. If the Chinese had been hoping that the Cuban crisis might reforge the unity of the bloc in the crucible of war they were bitterly disillusioned. Not only did Khrushchev back down over Cuba, but rather than risk losing Russia's carefully cultivated friendship with India, Khrushchev supported Nehru against Mao. From that moment the Sino-Soviet alliance was dead; Peiping recognized that it could no longer count upon the Soviet Union even for its security against the United States. The test ban treaty signaling the onset of the Soviet-American détente marked another stage in the rapidly deteriorating Sino-Soviet situation.

The ideological dispute over the necessity of war to advance socialism over peaceful coexistence, over "wars of national liberation," and over the possibility of advancing to socialism in the underdeveloped countries without resort to violence, had masked divergent national interests. There no longer being any possibility of reconciling Soviet and Chinese interests by agreement on principles, Peiping embarked upon a course of active competition with the Soviet Union for control of revolutionary movements everywhere.

On Chou En-lai's two-month tour of ten African states beginning in December 1963, the Chinese leader emphasized that China and Africa were committed to "the establishment of full independence and to the fight against imperialism, colonialism, and neo-colonialism" and that China, like Africa, was involved in "the common struggle against backwardness and economic development."[46] Russia by implication is a "have-nation" and even an imperialist power. Chou, inferentially at least, taxed the Soviet Union with giving at best "second priority to the liberation of colonial peoples, preferring an accommodation with the imperialist West," and with employing "typically imperialist methods in dealing with small states, interfering in their internal affairs and seeking to dictate to them."[47] This at a moment when Moscow was finding itself less and less able to command the obedience of Romania or for that matter of any of its European satellites.

More important from the American point of view Peiping has embarked upon a policy of active support for wars of national liberation and against those neighbors such as India that stand in the way of China's influence in Asia. By skillfully blending U.S. resistance to wars of national liberation and Afro-Asian prejudice against America, China hopes to identify the United States as the "gendarme of the world" and isolate it politically and strategically.

[46] Scalapino, Robert, "Sino-Soviet Competition in Africa," *Foreign Affairs*, Vol. 42, No. 4, July 1964, p. 641.

[47] *Ibid.*, p. 642.

CHAPTER 5

The Present Prospect

THE COMING TO OFFICE of President Johnson did not mark any immediate change in American foreign policy. Lyndon B. Johnson had established for himself the reputation as the country's greatest professional politician. He quickly showed his mastery of the domestic scene by rekindling confidence in the country's institutions (somewhat shaken by Kennedy's assassination) and by using his exceptional political talents to secure the passage of a much needed civil rights law.

The President maneuvered with caution in foreign affairs. He inherited a vastly improved military establishment under the direction of Secretary of Defense McNamara, as well as the talents of other men appointed during the Kennedy Administration such as Dean Rusk and McGeorge Bundy. During his first year in office Johnson was not called upon to make any major foreign policy decisions except, perhaps, in Viet Nam where the determination to continue existing policy was tantamount to a deepening of America's commitment.

It was not until after the November 1964 election that Johnson's decisions provided a clearer indication of his ultimate approach. The candidacy of Senator Barry Goldwater, the Republican presidential nominee, did not force Johnson to make any startling or original commitments in foreign affairs. Johnson's principal foreign policy plank was that the country needed a responsible finger on the nuclear button. With his election to the presidency, Johnson took firm control of United States foreign policy.

Another important change of government occurred in 1964. Khrushchev was supplanted as Soviet leader by Leonid Brezhnev who assumed the post of First Secretary of the Party and by Alexi Kosygin who became Premier. The new men continued Soviet support of a policy of détente in spite of the Viet Nam crisis; they have reserved their strictures almost exclusively for Washington's German policy.

Soviet-American Relations: Détente

The Cold War has now continued for twenty years. The détente that presently prevails in Soviet-American relations is a fragile and pathetic thing considering the potential for destruction and the issues that still remain unresolved between the two superpowers. Military competition continues as evidenced by the United States Air Force's efforts to put a vehicle into space that will provide a space platform for potential military use. The Soviets are doubtless engaged in similar projects. Nevertheless, given the extent of the revolution that has occurred in world relations in the past two decades and the possibilities for war that have existed, it is no mean accomplishment for the two superpowers to have avoided the ultimate of a nuclear holocaust. The United States has met the Soviet challenge on a series of shifting fronts and at various levels of violence. The challenge to political thought and action has been enormous. Just to cite some of the transformations suggests the magnitude of the revolution. The European legacy of three centuries of empire-building has been liquidated and scores of new nations—half-formed and ill-equipped for national existence—have sprung into being. The world has learned to live with nuclear weapons and missiles. In the process the two superpowers have taken the measure of each other's strengths and weaknesses, and they have found their efforts to undo each other unavailing. Without abandoning their hopes and their efforts to fragment the capitalist world, the Soviets have evidently come to conclude that they too have a stake in a limited détente with the Western powers. How long such a détente will endure is unknown. But much can be learned from the experience of the past twenty years to prepare us for the next twenty.

There are a number of reasons commonly given why the Soviet Union desired a détente: first, the previous record of failure in policies based on intimidation culminating in the failure of the Berlin Crisis of 1961 and Cuban Missile Crisis of October 1962; second, the evident inability of the Soviet Union to overtake the United States in strategic power at Russia's present level of economic prowess; third, the urgent need to economize on defense spending in order to finance and develop other sectors of the Soviet economy; fourth, the weight of the quarrel with China, which reinforces the Soviet belief that they will have more room for maneuver in the present world situation through a policy of détente than one of pressure and threat. Divisions within the North Atlantic community certainly further the Soviet objective of weakening NATO; and the Soviets would not wish to reforge that alliance by adopting a menacing posture. Finally, with the fall of Khrushchev, the new leaders have an additional reason to avoid foreign risks until the succession problem is settled. There has always been a strong latent desire for détente within the United States despite the earlier calls for the elimination of world Communism and the liberation of Eastern Europe from the Soviet yoke.

In Senator Fulbright's words, by the test-ban treaty "each side in effect assured the other that it was prepared to forego, at least for the present, any bid for a decisive military or political breakthrough."[1] Offsetting the present détente is the fact that none of the changes so far registered have any great bearing on the substance of the Cold War. The primordial questions upon which the issues of peace or war turn are simply being held in abeyance. Profound issues of security and status are still bound up in the unsettled questions of Berlin, of Germany, and of Eastern Europe.

The détente itself is potentially productive of a renewal of the tension at all the places mentioned above plus others as yet unknown. Here is how C. B. Marshall describes the dilemma confronting the statesman:

> However simple in its logical essences, the problem imposed by the double task which the United States has been essaying–maintaining the Alliance intact, or even improving it, and simultaneously seeking détente —is difficult in practical terms. The purposes tend to come into contradiction. The reason for having combined lies in the outsider's hostile intractability. To render him amicable and tractable removes the reason for combining. Lapse of motivation for combining relieves pressure on him to be tractable. . . . Such an alliance, moreover, is likely to be more unified on reasons for resisting than on terms for accommodating.[2]

The effort to achieve both a détente and preserve the alliance has, in Dean Acheson's apt phrase, put the United States in the position of a man both trying to blow and swallow at the same time; ". . . notwithstanding the declaratory aim of holding onto and even strengthening the Alliance while pushing initiatives for easement with the adversary—considerations integral to the Alliance framework are concomitantly downgraded."[3]

European-American Relations

Of the three European powers most intimately affected by recent trends in Soviet-American and Alliance relationships Great Britain

[1] *The New York Times,* March 26, 1964.

[2] C. B. Marshall, *The Exercise of Sovereignty* (Baltimore: Johns Hopkins, 1965), pp. 157–158.

[3] *Ibid.,* p. 158.

presents the least trouble. The United Kingdom is so thoroughly at one with the United States in its pursuit of détente as to pose virtually no problem. The same is obviously not true of France or West Germany.

France has complex and compelling reasons for breaking with the Alliance in its present hierarchical form. First, it objects to American dominance in principle, and second, de Gaulle's program for restoring France's importance in world affairs centers on gaining for France "a franchise in nuclear matters at least equivalent to that disposed by the United Kingdom" and thereby being assured of equivalent bargaining weight in the councils of the mighty.[4]

It is quite clear that de Gaulle would pursue these goals despite their potentially disruptive effect upon the Alliance regardless of the détente. But the détente adds an additional impulsion and justification for French downgrading of NATO.

The détente implies precisely that condition against which de Gaulle is in revolt—namely a Soviet-American agreement reached over the heads of and possibly at the expense of their respective allies.

> The principals in the nuclear cartel (Russia and the U.S.A.) reflecting a strategic equilibrium consonant with nuclear stalemate are seen as (seeking to restrain France's acquisition of a nuclear capability and as) arbiters over the future of Europe. Mutuality of understanding . . . takes on a character of entente.[5]

The more fully Soviet-American relations assume the form of a détente, the more logical appears de Gaulle's argument that Europe cannot count on America for the defense of its vital interests, and therefore the greater the need for an independent European nuclear strike force. In addition, the more one assumes that the Soviet Union is on the verge of being converted to détente the less reprehensible becomes the French "ally's desire to hedge its position" even at the expense of the alliance.[6]

The impact of détente upon West Germany is even more fundamental and more complex. West Germany's stake in the Alliance has always involved more than a security guarantee. Ever since

[4] *Ibid.*, p. 160.
[5] *Ibid.*, p. 158.
[6] *Ibid.*, p. 161.

Adenauer and the Western foreign ministers struck their 1951 bargain giving West Germany a virtual veto over future East-West negotiations, Bonn has had a stake in the alliance as a means of retrieving its lost unity and lost provinces. Détente immediately put the previously envisaged modes of unifying Germany into doubt.

Perhaps the indefinite postponement of German unification is something that must be accepted in the short- and middle-run for the sake of its long-run attainment fostered through the trends presently at work in Eastern Europe. Détente that involves an agreement to accept the status quo of a divided Germany need not mean, as C. B. Marshall suggests, that "Germany's status would descend implicitly to that of an ex-enemy country again," or that the Soviet Union "would be shown to hold the keys to Germany's future."[7] The assertions of national self-interest currently operating in Eastern Europe put a quite different complexion upon Russia's ability to hold the keys to Germany's future. It is with these imponderables as well as with changes in West Germany's perspective that we must concern ourselves. Simply to say that we cannot forgo any alteration in the scenario, vague as it has always been, for the reunification of Germany, for the sake of preserving NATO in the rigid and limited form that it acquired fifteen years ago is to run in the face of trends that neither we nor the Russians fully control.

Critics of the adverse impact that the détente has had upon the Alliance and especially upon German solidarity usually cite the West Germans' feeling that they have been misled, that having committed themselves body and soul to the West, they now find themselves unable to count upon achieving unity on Western terms. But was that ever a realistic assumption? Did Russia hold the key to German unity any less at the peak of the Cold War and under the system of rigid bipolarity than it does today? The trends in Europe that the United States did almost nothing to alter during the decade of 1955–1965 were bound sooner or later to bring out into the open what C. B. Marshall calls

> . . . the bare bones of logical possibilities for settlement in Europe-Soviet retraction, leaving the Alliance triumphant; United States retraction, leaving the Soviet Union encamped; reciprocal retraction by interpositions by both sides; and reciprocal acquiescence in existing lines, legitimizing zones of authority and influence as they are.[8]

[7] *Ibid.,* p. 162.
[8] *Ibid.,* p. 161.

True, the Soviet Union has encouraged and stands to profit from the consequences of these trends but it would have been better to have done something about them when it was still possible, and not lament about them afterward. There never was any hope of Germany being reunified under the bipolar system. Marshall laments:

> Yet for the Federal Republic to be associated as an ally in a decision disposing the future of Germany as a whole is logically and practically incompatible with terms likely to be conceded by the Soviet Union in circumstances short of a determinative defeat of its purposes in Central Europe. With respect to Germany, one sees how soon the course of détente comes to dead end—how soon exploration for possibilities of mutual gain must play out.[9]

It is certainly true that the détente has not enlarged the bargaining possibilities over Berlin or Germany nor ended the confrontation. The purpose of enlisting Germany in NATO was to hold the line of containment, and the West promised German unity without really believing that it could be secured. Because the détente has exposed the hollowness of that profession of purpose does not mean "a bargain by the paramount powers, the principals of the nuclear cartel over the sharing of Germany,"[10] on the model of Yalta. Such a bargain is no longer theirs to make, and it certainly does not mean that the future of Germany is permanently frozen into a divided state any more than it did at the height of the Cold War. The détente is the product of trends on both sides of the Iron Curtain. The United States and even West Germany have a stake in what those trends produce in the Eastern Zone. Zbigniew Brzezinski goes as far as to propose that the United States start treating the nations of Eastern Europe and their governments as genuinely sovereign entities so as to "breed national pride" among them and to stimulate their self-interest and political independence with an all-European economic development plan. The only country we should ostracize is East Germany, the only true satellite left, according to Brzezinski, while working for a Polish-West German rapprochement. Brzezinski would rule out any recognition of the East German regime in return for some regularization of Allied access to Berlin as was considered in the early 1960's.[11] This idea is imaginative but improbable *except* as part of natural, long-run developments knitting Eastern and Western Europe. For the present, détente means reciprocal acquiescence in existing lines,

[9] *Ibid.*, p. 162.
[10] *Ibid.*, p. 161.
[11] Brzezinski, Z., *Alternative to Partition* (New York: McGraw-Hill, 1965).

legitimizing zones of authority and influence as they are, but it need not and probably will not reduce West Germany to the position of a vanquished country. What happens to German-American relations and Soviet-American relations will be influenced by the caliber of United States statecraft in dealing with the whole question of North Atlantic and European relations. They cannot any longer be segmented nor can they be reduced to preserving the German question, the sheet anchor of NATO, in an unchanging and unyielding form.

Perhaps nothing has contributed so much to the transition in Soviet-American relationships as the breakup of the blocs. The blocs were the political engines of the Cold War. They had been brought into being for security reasons as a function of the naked polarity of power that existed at the war's end. Other nations mortgaged, or had mortgaged for them, their national will and independence either to Moscow or Washington in return for security and the physical survival of their societies. By the mid-1950's the extreme of weakness and terror had passed and various members of both blocs sought to reinterpret and reorient bloc relations in directions favorable to their own national interests. Failing that, they have simply begun to break away—as in the case of Red China and France. Neither bloc leader has been able to stem the transformation. Each has conducted elaborate campaigns to win back bloc unity under their respective leaderships. Moscow has waged an elaborate campaign first to placate and then to isolate China and at the same time to minimize the damage that Peiping has done to Russia's leadership of the world Communist movement; the United States has been engaged for the past five years in the same elaborate procedures toward Europe.

In the year or two before his death Kennedy was preoccupied with restoring American leadership over the North Atlantic Alliance in a new form. Equal partnership between a united Europe and the United States was the formula, with the understanding, of course, that Europe, if united, would "be outward looking," "a liberal trader and a reasonable negotiating partner willing to shoulder burdens of the alliance and to tailor her policies to the broader concept of a free world."[12] But partnership implies an identity of interests that simply has not existed apart from a common interest in defending against Soviet power.

The truth of the matter seems to be that Europe and the United

[12] Martin, Laurence W., "Europe and the Future of the Grand Alliance," in *Foreign Policy in the Sixties,* Hilsman and Goods (eds.), (Baltimore: Johns Hopkins Press, 1965) p. 29.

States are destined to move apart rather than together. "The United States has a global role peculiar to itself, in which it has no presently conceivable equal partner, and in which for the moment its only true opposite number is the Soviet Union."[13] Europe is a composite of several states that, whether united or divided, have distinctively European interests.[14]

The concept of two equal partners presupposes that each would adjust its behavior to accommodate the other. But has America ever been ready for such a partnership? When Washington spoke of equal partnership it never had any real intention of "trammeling its formal independence or reducing itself to merely an Atlantic partner. That is to say that, although the United States would like a firm arch between the two pillars to constrain Europe from using its newly united power in ways inimical to American interests, it is unwilling to restrict its own freedom reciprocally. Traffic on the arch would be one-way."[15] But Europe is reacting against this talk of equal partnership and twin pillars, precisely because it is based upon nothing more substantial than America's desire to keep things the way they are. But reality is much stronger than wishes. The Europeans would not be striking out on their own if they were not confident that they can take care of themselves vis-a-vis the Soviet Union. The United States will retain its role as a diplomatic participant but as Professor Laurence Martin suggests, "It is difficult not to conclude that dominant American leadership (in Europe) is henceforth inevitably open to question and that solutions centered around the Atlantic alone, especially on federalist models, are both remote and of doubtful merit."[16]

Kennedy's effort to bridge the widening gulf between Europe and Washington had been the Multilateral Nuclear Force—an essentially military expedient. American efforts to sell the MLF to the Europeans quickly became embarrassing because it added to the military confusion without solving the problem of European control. True, the biggest single stumbling block was de Gaulle, but his opposition alone was sufficient to deter the other European states from giving it anything but a perfunctory reception. Instead of pushing a plan that was violently opposed by de Gaulle and that held out no solution whatsoever to the psychological and political gulf opening up between the United States and Europe, President Johnson wisely dropped it.

[13] *Ibid.*, p. 31.
[14] *Ibid.*, p. 30.
[15] *Ibid.*, p. 31.
[16] *Ibid.*, p. 32.

Johnson has quietly allowed the old "special relationship" between Britain and the United States to reassert itself without giving undue offense to France. The North Atlantic Treaty Organization continues to provide a framework for United States military presence in Europe, which is still cherished by the other European capitals if not by Paris. If French and American diplomatic interests were to diverge too completely it is conceivable that France might withdraw from NATO, but Johnson appears to have avoided the likelihood of such an ultimate split by quietly burying MLF and not making NATO a source of irritation between the United States and France. Nothing has happened or need happen in European-American relations to weaken the credibility of the American nuclear deterrent, unless the United States wants it to be lessened, which would be self-defeating. No European statesman, not even de Gaulle, has rejected the necessity for continued military cooperation within the framework of the North Atlantic Treaty. There is no reason why a loose integration of British and French nuclear forces, "formally independent but in practice increasingly integrated as a specialized contribution to common power"[17] could not be worked out. Such an arrangement may now have to await de Gaulle's passing from the scene.

The future of Europe, which shone so hopefully at the beginning of the 1960's has become more and more clouded by de Gaulle's machinations. The more successful he has been at excluding Britain and America from the life of the Inner Six the more apparent it has become that he "wants for Europe exactly what he abhors for the Atlantic Community: the hegemony of a single nuclear power."[18]

In his obsession with maintaining his and France's status, de Gaulle may have increased French bargaining power in the short run, but what of the longer run? By itself France cannot seriously hope to compete with the continental powers—Russia and America—in the nuclear and ICBM sphere. By "reducing the Common Market to a technical organization from which his ministers (are) able to draw every advantage for the French economy, while chopping down the political hopes of its creators," de Gaulle has prevented Europe from achieving that degree of unity which alone will enable it to compete with Russia and America.[19] By his behavior de Gaulle has released

[17] *Ibid.*, p. 33.

[18] Mehnert, Klaus, "European Unity: A German View" in *Détente,* edited by Dulles, E. L. and Crane, R. D. (Praeger: New York, 1965), p. 209.

[19] Luthy, Herbert, "De Gaulle: Pose and Policy," in *Foreign Affairs,* July, 1965, p. 570.

Germany from much of that sense of obligation to the rest of Europe upon which the unity and stability of Western Europe depend. While de Gaulle explores "the foggy perspectives of a 'European Europe' equilibrated between Paris and Moscow," West Germany is losing its patience.[20] The danger is that de Gaulle has unsettled Europe more than he realizes and that the forces he is unleashing may come back to haunt France.

Sino-American Relations

If a détente exists in Soviet-American relations the same cannot be said to be true of Sino-American relations. In a sense the United States is experiencing with China what it has gone through with the Soviet Union. The rulers of China are imbued with a messianic fervor and a deep sense of dissatisfaction with the prevailing balance of power in Asia. From the very beginning of Communist rule in China Peiping has made it clear that it had no desire to negotiate with the United States, especially not for the purpose of stabilizing a status quo in Asia, which does not suit Chinese interests. The immediate Chinese objective is to establish a Monroe Doctrine for Asia.

> This scheme implies three major principles: (1) exclusion of all Western influence from Asia, including the influence of the United States and the Soviet Union; (2) settlement of Asian affairs by Asians; and (3) hegemony of Communist China over the area. . . . For several reasons Indochina is the most significant place to realize those objectives at the moment.[21]

As a result of the war in Korea and in Viet Nam the United States accepted commitments in Asia that shifted the balance even more unfavorably to the People's Republic of China.

Above and beyond national interest the leadership in Peiping is motivated by ideological imperatives. They are convinced that there exists a revolutionary potential in the world which as Communists they must liberate in order to smash the evil of imperialism. Furthermore, drawing upon their own revolutionary experience, the Chinese Communists believe that they have discovered a new, potent, and surefire tactic in the form of "internal wars" waged through guerrillas and organized terrorism. They are sufficiently cautionary to prefer to work through a third party and Hanoi, in pursuit of its own interests

[20] *Ibid.*, p. 571.

[21] Chen, King, "Peking's Strategy in Indochina," *Yale Review,* Summer, 1965, p. 550.

against South Viet Nam, has provided Peiping with just the means to smash, humiliate, and defeat the United States without great risk to itself.

> Geographically (Indochina) provides an excellent strategic base for expanding the Communist movement to the rest of Southeast Asia. Economically it has a large surplus of rice, which China needs. Ideologically, it offers an opportunity to prove to the Communist parties of the world that Peking's strategy of crushing Western imperialism is superior to the Soviet strategy of peaceful coexistence.[22]

In a sense the United States-China conflict is the Asian analogue of the twenty years' struggle with the Soviet Union. The United States is attempting to contain Communist expansion by meeting it at all levels. It hopes at the same time to educate Peiping to the facts of international life in the nuclear age before China acquires a nuclear capability of its own, under cover of which it might mistakenly embark upon a course leading to all-out war.

America's campaign to isolate China has been as much ideological and emotional in inspiration as strategic. American efforts fall in with Peiping's own campaign to represent America's role in Asia as that of an imperialist interloper determined to keep Asia down. By persisting in this attitude the United States merely feeds a deep-running strain of moral self-righteousness in Peiping's attitude without denying China access to the foodstuffs and strategic resources of the non-Communist world of deterring Chinese operations in Southeast Asia.

In the present stage of the struggle the United States is motivated by the fear that if China were to succeed in its support for wars of national liberation and if the Viet Cong succeeded in winning power, the least that would occur would be a swing of Asian countries into the Chinese orbit and at worst, revolutionary movements would spring up in other underdeveloped countries intent upon making good their claim to power by violence. The outbreak of war between India and Pakistan over Kashmir in September 1965 was a manifestation of the instability against which the United States is seeking to guard. At the same time the United States is concerned for the side effects, should China succeed, upon Soviet behavior. The Soviet-American détente rests in part at least upon the Soviet belief that nothing is to be gained at the present juncture that would be worth the price of worsening relations with the United States or abetting Peiping; but if

[22] *Ibid.*, pp. 550–551.

China succeeded in demonstrating the effectiveness of wars of national liberation carried out by means of guerrilla movements and terrorism Moscow might find itself obliged to compete.

In October 1964 the Chinese exploded their first atomic bomb introducing a portentous new factor into world politics. The principal motivation China gave for its action was the desire for a more credible deterrent against an American attack.

> This is a major achievement of the Chinese people in their struggle to increase their national defense capability and oppose the United States imperialist policy of nuclear blackmail and nuclear threats.[23]

The Chinese also made it clear that they intend to exploit the bomb for whatever additional influence it would give them within the Communist bloc, to support wars of national liberation, and to enhance Chinese hegemony in Asia. It is in the latter context that China's A-bomb may yield the greatest results "reminding the countries of Asia of the presence on their borders of a major military power. . . ."[24] Of course this may prompt Japan and India, two states capable of developing A-bombs, to put aside their aversion to nuclear weapons and embark on atom bomb projects of their own.

Because of China's present vulnerability the immediate struggle against American imperialism proceeds "not by direct confrontation but indirectly—that is to say on the territory of third parties—whether the means employed are political, economic, or military."[25] The most promising situations in which to push the struggle have been in Viet Nam and Laos.

South Viet Nam provides an ideal terrain for Communist China to try out the efficacy of "internal war" and perhaps deliver a blow at "United States imperialism." There is no evidence that at the time the United States became engaged in South Viet Nam or for several years thereafter that Washington anticipated the kind of war that it now confronts there. The American perspective at the time was "linesmanship" in which it was assumed that if we drew a line and gave it United States backing we could make it immune from Communist assault. The fact that South Viet Nam was an artificial creation with

[23] Quoted in *The New York Times,* October 17, 1964, p. 10.

[24] Halperin, Morton, "China and the Bomb," *The China Quarterly,* No. 21, January–March, 1965, p. 81.

[25] Halpern, A. M., "China in the Postwar World," *The China Quarterly,* No. 21, January–March, 1965, p. 41.

an ineffective government dependent upon United States backing made it an ideal target for political and guerrilla warfare, which North Viet Nam was only too willing to sponsor. For all its much vaunted understanding of insurgency the United States consistently underestimated the liabilities that the local government bears in confronting a guerrilla war:

> responsibility for maintaining order, not in one or two spots but everywhere in the country, not against open operations but against treachery, assassination, sabotage, hit-and-run attacks by unknown individuals who melt back, unidentifiable, into their own village backgrounds. . . .[26]

By 1964 the situation had so far deteriorated that the Viet Cong moved virtually at will in the countryside; the Viet Cong soon constituted a virtual state within a state governing and collecting taxes and raising forces over a large portion of the countryside.

By the beginning of 1965 the hope that South Viet Nam could be saved without direct, major United States military involvement had to be abandoned. Rather than let the country collapse, the United States began bombing missions against military targets in North Viet Nam and thousands of American ground forces were being sent into South Viet Nam to salvage what could be salvaged from the debacle. The United States obviously regards the war in Viet Nam as a test of wills in which if the Communists win, Peiping will have given a dangerous demonstration of the efficacy of "internal wars" fought through guerrillas and organized terrorism. Furthermore it is assumed that a Viet Cong victory would have disastrous repercussions on the rest of Southeast Asia. Already Cambodia and Laos are virtually in the Chinese Communist orbit and Burma and Indonesia are teetering on the brink. Whether the United States would have chosen this particular terrain on which to fight had its prestige and power not already been engaged in South Viet Nam is a moot point.

The Viet Cong war in Viet Nam is a highly unfortunate type of confrontation upon which the United States has been forced to have the issue turn, although under the circumstances it may have had no other choice. It is unfortunate in the first place because a war fought in the jungles of Asia against guerrilla forces is not one that can be easily won; second, the political disadvantages to the United States

[26] Watson, Mark S., Review of Galula, David, *Counterinsurgency Warfare Theory and Practice. Political Science Quarterly,* Vol. LXXX, No. 2, June 1965, pp. 324–325.

of escalation are enormous; third, it is a war that, even if we do not lose, is not likely to contribute much to the overall stability and security of Southeast Asia in the manner that success against the Greek guerrillas inspired resolution and confidence in Europe. Finally, the war might have the unfortunate consequence of bringing about a rupture of the détente should the Soviet Union feel obliged to choose between support for the Viet Cong or being stigmatized before the world Communist movement as "revisionists" and "class collaborators."

The Johnson Administration seems to be aware of these considerations. Present strategy appears to be to intensify the pressure upon the Viet Cong and upon Hanoi in the hope that some change will occur in Hanoi's attitude toward the war which would make possible negotiations. Hanoi settled for less than the whole loaf in 1954; it may be willing to do so again. Then again Hanoi may feel that it was deprived of the fruits of its victory in 1954, and this may stiffen its opposition to anything less than total victory.

Meanwhile what of the larger issues of Chinese-American relations? Professor Halpern notes that at present some of China's objectives are "inherently nonrational, as are other people's. . . . It appears that the CCP to some extent evaluates its actions in terms of a judgment of how they will contribute to the complete liquidation of imperialism."[27] In appraising the Chinese Communists it also is important to note that while they are not reckless neither are they cautious.

> A truly cautious man is not only prudent in his procedures but tends to direct himself to the safer rather than the maximum options . . . When the stakes are high and the threat is imminent, the Chinese are capable of putting everything at risk.[28]

With this in mind it is clear that if the worst is to be avoided in Sino-American relations two adjustments must take place—one Chinese and one American. The United States must be willing to recognize China's claim to a great-power status in Asia, and Peiping must purge itself of the nonrational belief that it must exorcise the world of "imperialist devils," i.e., the United States. This double adjustment may be as crucial to the history of the next twenty years as the adjustments in Soviet-American relations have been to that of the past twenty.

[27] Halpern, *op. cit.,* p. 44.
[28] *Ibid.,* p. 45.

United States Relations with the Third World

The gap between the revolution of rising expectations and the actual conditions of life over much of the Afro-Asian and Latin American world is so great that change, when it comes, has the force and violence of revolution. The advanced industrial countries can help them through the throes of economic and cultural change but they cannot save them from the experience itself. The ethic of work and discipline and adherence to the impersonal and rational processes of modern economic life demand a reshaping of the personality. The transformation of the personality and of the traditional culture in the crucible of change is a searing and traumatic experience for which no substitute has yet been found precisely because it is so personal.

We are entering an era of maximum revolutionary upheaval. Because of the form that these revolutions are likely to take and because of Communism's avowed intention to exploit these movements to isolate and smash the "imperialist" system of the United States, critics of American foreign policy, such as Hans Morgenthau, have been concerned that the Johnson Administration is in danger of believing that the United States "can oppose all revolutionary movements around the world" and that "we shall then transform ourselves into the anti-revolutionary power per se after the model of Metternich's Austria of 150 years ago, and we will find ourselves defending a status quo which we know to be unjust and in the long run indefensible."[29] Morgenthau argues that we are in the process of adopting this strategy because our foreign policy has taken for its standard "the active hostility to a world wide political movement . . . Communism" which "confuses the sphere of philosophic or moral judgment with the realm of political action and for this reason it is bound to fail."[30]

These criticisms of American policy were prompted not only by the United States' actions in Viet Nam but also by the President's decision to land the Marines in the Dominican Republic to avoid any possibility that Communists or Castroites might come to the fore in the wake of a popular revolution against an incumbent military junta. Critics saw in Johnson's action the crowning proof that he had abandoned the Kennedy approach in favor of the more conservative Mann approach, named after Undersecretary of State, Thomas

[29] Morgenthau, Hans, "Globalism," *The New Republic,* July 3, 1965, p. 22.
[30] *Ibid.,* p. 21.

Mann. Many observers claim that the alleged Communist influence in the Dominican uprising was negligible and that the United States damaged its reputation by violating the provisions of the Organization of American States forbidding unilateral intervention. A more important issue, one that has been obscured by reference to nineteenth century standards of international conduct, is whether or not the superpowers can afford to rest their security on the turn of a revolution in some minuscule and traditionally ill-governed state. A Castro type of regime can pose a deadly threat to United States security as was evident in the Cuban missile crisis. Morgenthau and other critics of U.S. policy are still looking at events through nineteenth century eyes even though they recognize the enormous difference that two world wars as well as thermonuclear and missile technology have brought about in the ability of the nation-state to offer its citizens security. Can the United States or the Soviet Union, confronted as they are by worldwide problems of great complexity, afford to risk upsetting their external or internal equilibrium by the interplay of factions in petty republics? Has the time not come when the lesser powers would be advised to get together and arrange their affairs on some basis that would not give cause to a neighboring great power to intervene? Dag Hammarskjold sensed this when he remarked that it is little powers not superpowers that need the United Nations to uphold and order their interests.

The critics of American foreign policy do not tell us how to recognize when we are confusing hostility to an ideological movement with resistance within a legitimate sphere of political action. Those who defend what the United States is doing in Viet Nam argue that we are defending a strategic interest by being in Viet Nam and that we are not pursuing a course of moral crusadism. In South Viet Nam it is confronting the openly avowed strategy and tactic of Communist expansion by indirect aggression and internal war operating through the Viet Cong and Hanoi.

> The ultimate issue for us in South Vietnam, therefore, is not obscure, although it is disagreeable: it is to maintain the policy which former Ambassador George Kennan, 18 years ago, first labeled "Containment." Kennan's idea—that of mutual respect for the frontiers of the Communist and free worlds—is a necessary if not a sufficient condition of Peaceful Coexistence. It implies that we halt aggression at the boundaries of the Cold War as we did in Greece, Korea and Berlin, in the natural hope that the passage of time will reduce the danger of general war. It has been a demanding and wearisome policy. But it has kept the Cold War within tolerable limits and has helped to preserve nuclear peace.
>
> In Indochina the North Vietnamese government has broken the first and

most basic rule of Peaceful Coexistence: that the frontiers of the two systems not be altered unilaterally, or by military action. To cite a clear parallel, it has been deemed self-evident in Washington and in Moscow that it would be unthinkably dangerous for either East Germany or West Germany to attack the other, either openly or through infiltration. Yet what North Vietnam, with Chinese backing, is attempting in Indochina—to conquer a country the United States has agreed to protect—is the precise analogue of such a hypothetical German conflict, or of the Korean war of 1950–53, or of the Soviet Union's early postwar probes against Greece, Turkey and Iran.

The Communist movement, now turbulent with rivalry for leadership, is seeking to enlarge its area of control, especially by rushing into the near-vacuums of power in the new countries of Asia and Africa and identifying itself with their aspirations for progress. The Western nations, and notably the United States, have sought to counter this outward thrust of the Communist movement and to help the nonindustrialized countries master the secrets of modern wealth. Both sides have shown prudence in a series of moves and ripostes. These have helped to define not a new international law but a pattern of custom, an understood rule-of-the-game-of-Cold-War, from which new law might grow.[31]

It may well be that the most damning criticism against United States' policy is not about its ends but about its means. Critics like Walter Lippmann contend that the United States cannot hope to preserve the balance by fighting a jungle war in Southeast Asia; that we can only hope to preserve the balance where our formidable air and naval power can be effective. Others point to the wretched record of successive American-backed regimes in Saigon and wonder why more was not done in such a critical undertaking to overcome the corruption that has undermined our position. They argue that the United States cannot enter into such engagements devoid of the will and the means to cope with a guerrilla struggle that is more political than military. The chief lesson of Viet Nam ought to be that a unilateral, two-dimensional strategy for containing Communism in the vulnerable parts of Asia, Africa, and Latin America is not sufficient. The United States must make even clearer than it has in the past that its objective in Asia and elsewhere is not to build up anti-Communist bastions for the sake of attacking China but to preserve the integrity of the area. It must also be more candid in recognizing what it takes to defend a weak and vulnerable society against a shrewdly conceived political and terrorist assault. It can scarcely be said that America's nonrecognition policy and unilateralist incursions into Southeast Asia constituted such an approach. Although

[31] Rostow, Eugene V., "The Realities of Power Demand that We Must Fight On," *Life,* July 2, 1965, p. 40B.

nothing can be done without American will and power, Peiping has found it easy to isolate and identify America in many Asian minds as a new form of Western imperialism. This unilateralist style has also been the single most disturbing characteristic of the Dominican decision.

In the case of Asia any calculation of our strategic interest and of our policy at the point of decision must include a recognition of the full weight that Chinese influence is bound to have in the region and of the strategic and tactical limits to America's capacity to offset that weight. If then it is still deemed strategically necessary to intervene to maintain the balance of power, then we would do so with intelligent forethought.

There is a danger of confusing the strategic and political purpose for our being in Viet Nam or for our action in the Dominican Republic with the inadequacy or inappropriateness of our means. We may well be wise in our intention of defending the balance of power in Southeast Asia long enough for the non-Communist states of that region to master their destiny and chart their own course for Asia, but wrong in our assessment of our own capacity to do so. We may have been mistaken in our general policy toward Red China and right now in our strategy toward the situation in Viet Nam. Whether the present debacle was avoidable or whether Hanoi and Peiping would have pursued their present policy regardless of what we had done to avoid it is a moot question. We are now confronted with stark and unappealing alternatives requiring the coolest and most detached consideration of alternatives.

To be driven from Viet Nam because we either did not possess or did not exercise in time the means of holding it is no dishonor, talk of prestige notwithstanding. The line will have to be drawn somewhere else under more or less disadvantageous circumstances. Although Southeast Asia is not a "core interest" of the United States, as one of two superpowers with worldwide responsibilities the United States has a vital interest in the security of Southeast Asia. It is not an interest that the United States can abdicate any more than it can abdicate its interest in the Caribbean, Berlin, Korea; or Turkey. Therefore, pulling out of Viet Nam may become a necessity imposed upon us as an alternative to enlarging a war that we cannot hope to win by conventional means, but defeat will not end the involvement of American power in the area. Sooner or later the last resort of power must set limits to the expansion of Chinese domination into Southeast Asia. The particular form that the balance takes may be a mixture of regimes running from protégés like North Viet Nam and dependencies like Cambodia to fully independent regimes such as those of Thailand and India. But in their sum they must set some form of limit to Chinese power or the alternative will be war on a major scale.

In achieving this political goal the United States cannot rely upon military means alone, nor upon economic aid. In the conduct of its diplomacy the United States must be conscious of that "middle ground of subtle distinctions, complex choices, and precarious manipulations, which is the proper sphere of foreign policy."[32]

The twenty years since the end of World War II have witnessed a further evolution of the Communist system from a bearer of a universalist ideology energized by the belief in an imminent and favorable culmination of historical processes and determined to overturn the Western state system toward something akin to the Western state system itself. The failure of Communism to sustain its universalist pretention is, as Edward Buehrig says, due "to the irrepressible interests that cling to the particular, resisting absorption in the universal. Russia and China have not escaped the elemental frictions of politics. . . . Moreover, the states of Eastern Europe have retained their national identities and have asserted themselves against the suffocating embrace of Moscow. . . .[33]

Although mistakes of temper and detail are freely charged against the West:

> It is noteworthy that external resistance to the expansion of communism has failed to induce unity and central authority within the (Communist) movement. Actually interaction between communism and the Western State System has eroded, not the prevailing (nation-state) system, but the universal proclivities of communism itself . . . . communism has been obliged to conform to the pattern of diplomatic relations between equals, employing it even within its own sphere.[34]

This is an historic transformation of no mean significance, accomplished under often desperate circumstances without resort to a general war. The West now faces its analogue in the ambitions of Communist China but with the Communist world rent by schism.

The dilemma now is to give form and order to that vast proliferation of nation-state formations that have been spawned in the past twenty years while holding the central balance. "The location of authority within and among societies is what politics is about" and never has this political problem "been so pervasive and so dangerous

[32] Morgenthau, *op. cit.*, p. 19.

[33] Buehrig, Edward H., "The Institutional Pattern of Authority," *World Politics*, Vol. XVII, No. 3. April 1965, p. 375.

[34] *Ibid.*, p. 375.

as today."[35] Form and order are lacking because over vast areas of the world the existing distribution of authority is unknown or unacceptable. Outside of the West great uncertainty and uneasiness prevails both about where authority lies within the state and between states. There is no consensus as to the authority of governments nor as to the identity of nations or existing boundaries in many parts of the world. With a number of these still unstable states about to acquire atomic technology, the future is rife with uncertainty and foreboding. Time is running out on any hopes that may have existed at the time of the test ban treaty of preventing the indiscriminate proliferation of nuclear weapons.

If the past twenty years have demonstrated anything, it is that neither Washington nor Moscow have had the legitimate authority or power to give form and order to the emergent world. International organization has been the most promising response of the twentieth century to the risks of international anarchy. Although it is true that "the goal of international peace and security . . . escapes the embrace of international organization, which has not in fact been able to control events,"[36] international organization is still the most apt instrument for tempering the shocks to which the diversity and multicentered freedom of the nation-state system give rise.

The United Nations has not performed the function envisaged for it at its inception—that of a great power consortium institutionalized in the Security Council for preserving order and providing for peaceful change. But the United Nations has survived the vicissitudes of the Cold War and emerged with a distinctive international role. It has

> . . . converted autonomous membership in the international community into something more significant than mere juridical novelty. As a third party, international organization has been active rather than passive. Though failing to materialize as a framework of order and justice, it has functioned as a new variable, interacting independently with the numerous factors comprising today's international politics. The contemporary situation, nineteen years after the Second World War, is significantly different from that prevailing at the comparable period after the First World War.[37]

Because the majority of United Nations members are emphatically anticolonialist and because the Communist bloc has a seeming monopoly on the anti-imperialist motif, the United States has hesitated to let the United Nations sit in judgment on its operations in Viet Nam, the Dominican Republic, and elsewhere. Because the bulk of the

[35] *Ibid.*, p. 376.
[36] *Ibid.*, p. 385.
[37] *Ibid.*, p. 385.

non-Western nations are neutralist in their orientation, and capable of adopting "a plague on both your houses" attitude toward Cold War issues considered of strategic importance by the United States, the latter hesitates to place such issues under the jurisdiction of the United Nations. But the stake that many of these new states already have and that others will acquire in the state-preserving and state-building function of the United Nations and in its potentiality for removing certain dangerous issues from the Cold War arena ought to be fostered and supported by the United States.

The United States has the greatest stake in developing a definition of indirect or subversionary aggression and a system of collective prevention and sanctions against such aggression. The Congo operation affords something of a model. The United States has neither the resources nor the authority to intervene in every revolution or conflict in which Communism is presumed to lurk or be at work. The United Nations as well as regional organizations such as the Organization of American States represent the best hope for providing such an authority. But unless the United States, which has a crucial stake in developing a normative order and peacekeeping machinery backs the United Nations and other regional organizations even at a risk to its own immediate interest, then the nation-state system is likely to degenerate toward anarchy.

In dealing with crises involving the Afro-Asian or Latin American sphere, the United States is at a grave disadvantage both because it is the power seeking to maintain order and because it is identified with European imperialism. It is all the more important, therefore, that it associate with, rather than contribute to the erosion of, the authority of the United Nations. Just as the critics of détente have been transfixed by fear for NATO into denying validity to new forces and trends, so they have scandalously misrepresented the causes for denying to the United Nations a major role in American strategy. There is a passing strange theory that contends that the major problems of international politics are caused by the small and inchoate powers. Thus C. B. Marshall writes: "The perils and perplexities of the world about us rise not so much from an excess of the constituent qualities of sovereignty in the entities passing as nation-states as from an entirely opposite circumstance,"[38] the implication being that the situation of major conflict between the Soviet Union and the United States and China is not the principal source of international tension. This view is like blaming a shaking of the jungle forest not upon the

[38] Marshall, C. B., *The Exercise of Sovereignty* (Baltimore: Johns Hopkins University Press, 1965), p. 5.

elephants passing below but upon the monkeys because they happen to be in the trees. Benjamin V. Cohen, who represented the United States at the United Nations from 1948 to 1952, has written that

> It is gravely disturbing that many devoted friends of the United Nations have failed to grasp that the U.N. is threatened with failure as much or more by the neglect of the great powers as by the irresponsibility of the small states . . . there is nothing in the Charter or outside the Charter that would justify the great powers any more than the small powers in rejecting or ignoring the conciliation, mediation, or other processes and procedures that the United Nations might provide for settlement of disputes. . . .[39]

This view does not imply or deny that a condition of balance between the great powers will continue to depend upon the adjustment of relations on a power political basis. But the United States at least has a stake in minimizing the range of issues over which it must stand ultimate guard and over which it might come into conflict with the Soviet Union. The United States can have no interest in seeing the international system degenerate into anarchy and violence—violence all the more deadly when a host of new powers have acquired nuclear weapons.

Conclusion

What can be said of the history of the past twenty years? What has been gained? The answer is "not much," but what little has been achieved is precious and important. The world has certainly not advanced by any measurable distance toward world law and order based upon either an emergent consensus or upon some transcendent principle or spirit of unity. The world is still organized into an imperfect system of national societies. One set of such societies, the Communist, impelled by the messianic dream of creating a more perfect system, has been tempted to overthrow the existing system; so far it has not been permitted to succeed. In 1947 the United States, not without much hesitancy and subsequent aberrations, stepped in to perform the essential balancing and containing function, which is the only fully developed principle of order the nation-state knows. The only previous experience the twentieth century has had with nation-state rivalries in a totalitarian age with weapons of mass destruction has been the plunge into World War I and the sickening retreat from responsibility leading inevitably, by way of appeasement, to the upheaval of World War II. One would be foolhardy to

[39] Cohen, Benj. V., "Using the United Nations," *The New Republic,* May 8, 1965, p. 14.

predict that the world of nation-states, subject as it continues to be to the corrosive force of insecurity and obliged to grapple with forces of incalculable obduracy, complexity, and unpredictability, can indefinitely escape the ultimate ordeal of general and possibly nuclear war. But the record of the past twenty years is a monument to what Dulles, in a less fortunate context, called the necessary art—of going to the brink without falling over. The interaction of the Cold War, of the weapons race, and of the revolution in the Third World has put almost superhuman burdens upon the statesmen in Moscow, Washington, London, Paris, and the lesser capitals. In a real sense the past twenty years have been a monument to man's tenacity to survive and to the blending of responsibility and power in a nightmarish setting. "As every nerve was strained in the struggle to survive, (as) the freedom to dissent became narrower, (as) every national energy was channeled into the war effort, and (as) the complex conception of reality . . . was forced to give way to the black and white patterns of the propagandist"[40] it was touch and go at times if the world would survive the contest. Somehow politics has managed to win through—the conviction that "though national self-interest is an inescapable reality it must not be accepted as normative."[41] Statesmen and peoples have somehow begun to learn—whether through reason or fear of the bomb—that a foreign policy which is not defined with respect for universal values or at least those of a civilization transcending that of the nation itself is not in the national interest. At Berlin, in Korea, in Cuba, and now in Viet Nam the proposition is being tested that "the 'necessities' in international politics, and for that matter in all spheres of life, do not push decisions and actions beyond the realm of moral judgment; they rest on moral choices themselves. If a statesman decides that the dangers to the security of his country are so great as to make necessary a course of action that may lead to war, he has placed an exceedingly high value on an increment of national security."[42]

Given the potential for disaster with which the world has had to wrestle for the past two decades, perhaps its most significant meaning may be found in the words of Abbé Sièyes when upon being asked what he had done during the French Revolution replied, "I survived."

[40] Sterling, Richard, "Political Necessity and Moral Principle in the Thought of Friedrich Meinecke," *Foreign Policy in the Sixties* edited by Hilsman, Roger, and Good, Robert. (Baltimore: Johns Hopkins University Press, 1965), p. 266.

[41] Good, Robert, "National Interest and Moral Theory," *Foreign Policy in the Sixties,* p. 273.

[42] Wolfers, Arnold, *Discord and Collaboration: Essays on International Politics* (Baltimore: Johns Hopkins University Press, 1962), p. 58.